Michael Buckley w[...] [...]
in 1924. He was [...]
sentation College, Cork and the Gregorian
University in Rome, where he gained his
Licentiate and Doctorate in Sacred
Theology. He was ordained there on 23rd
December 1950.

After working in the British Isles he re-
turned to Rome in 1954 as Inter in
Philosophy to the English College, and was
Professor of Philosophy at Beda College,
Rome from 1957 to 1960.

Between 1966 and 1977 he was director
of an ecumenical and pastoral centre at
Wetherby, the first of its kind in Europe,
which made a great impact on the
ecumenical scene. In 1968, Michael Buckley
was appointed Roman Catholic Religious
Advisor to Yorkshire Television and still
appears on many of their religious pro-
grammes, as well as on BBC's "Pause For
Thought".

Pope Paul VI appointed him to the
Vatican Secretariat for Promoting Christian
Unity, a position he held for five years from
1968, and he has continued this work
through his healing missions and material
help.

Monsignor Buckley has been Parish Priest
of St Joseph's Church, Tadcaster, Yorkshire,
but is now working full-time in the healing
ministry. He is the author of several books,
including *Let Peace Disturb You*, which is
also published by Fount.

MICHAEL BUCKLEY D. D.

His Healing Touch

A personal witness to the
power of God's healing love

Collins
FOUNT PAPERBACKS

First published by Fount Paperbacks, London in 1987
Second impression March 1989

© Michael Buckley 1987

Printed and bound in Great Britain by
William Collins Sons & Co. Ltd, Glasgow

Bible quotations are generally taken
from the *Jerusalem Bible*,
copyright © 1966, 1967 and 1968
by Darton, Longman & Todd Ltd (London)
and by Doubleday & Company, Inc (New York),
and are used by kind permission of the publishers

To my Father
whose Love heals me

Contents

Introduction

This is a book about healing. I never thought I would have written on such a subject, but it is the one book I know I must write. I might have chosen as the title *His Loving Touch*, but to have done so would have evaded the main theme about which I want to write, namely, healing. I believe in healing not so much because I have witnessed it in other people's lives but that I have experienced it in my own. Because God loves me he has healed me, and continues to heal me all through my life. The writing of this book is a very special healing for me. By choosing the title *His Healing Touch* I proclaim my totally committed belief in an all-powerful, all-merciful God, who as a Father heals his people. I hope this book will heal people of the many false theories and practices which divest healing of its true and rightful place in the life and mission of all Christians.

Healing is an evocative word. A very close friend of mine advised me, "Write about prayer, theology, anything you like, but for God's sake, don't write about healing, that's a real minefield." So the word itself, even before you can explain what you mean by it, generates all sorts of highly emotional and irrational reactions among Christians. If we cannot agree on what we are talking about, then is it any wonder that we disagree about its place in Christian life? The first healing we all need is to understand the nature and scope of healing. It could and should be a source of Christian unity and evangelical power. Sadly this is not so. What one Christian understands by healing as essential to the Gospel, and his growth as a Christian person, is anathema to another. As long as we are divided on healing then Christian unity will remain a pipe-dream, and the Gospel about man being fully human and fully alive will never be proclaimed in all its power.

Much of what passes for healing in Christian denominations other than my own disturbs my conscience, just as the lack of awareness of healing among many fellow Catholics is a source of deep personal pain. As a general rule our attitude to healing depends largely upon our type of churchmanship, background and culture. However, at times I am more "at home" in healing with some Christians of other denominations than I am with "my own". Healing is not the prescriptive right or sole possession of any denomination. It belongs to the Church of Christ, to those who believe in the power of the Holy Spirit at work in our world, continuing the reconciling and healing mission of Jesus Christ.

Right from the outset of this book I define as clearly as I can what I mean by healing. In many ways it is a purely personal belief but I know that it finds an echo in the minds and hearts of many Christians of widely differing denominations. I have chosen deliberately not to quote any celebrated "healers" or writers on healing. The only books I refer to are the gospels, which for me come alive in the healing ministry more than anywhere else. Any references to actual healings are mentioned only in so far as they illustrate and clarify a teaching which is sorely needed if healing is to be understood and practised correctly. In no way am I impressed with those books which are an exhaustive and exhausting recitation of one extraordinary physical healing after another. Healing is much more than physical healing. Healing for me is the *ordinary* will of a loving God for his children, and most of its effects on the human person, which are *internal*, are hidden from our human eyes and minds, which crave excessively for proof and confirmation of a Father's love already revealed in his only Son. Just as the best and only way to learn how to pray is to pray, so also with healing. Look inside yourself, see what God has done for you, thank him for it and then perhaps you will "know" what is meant by healing. Healing is basically a personal expérience. If you cannot find any instances in your life where God has proved himself a loving Father to you then this book has as little to say to you as a colour magazine has to a blind man.

For me healing is very much part and parcel of my Christian life. It is as natural to me as the air I breathe. God the Father wants me to live the life of his risen Son, and gives me all the means necessary to do it. He heals me in my wounded self and world. So by healing I mean simply that as a person living in a world damaged by sin Christ heals my relationships with my Father, my neighbour and within myself. Healing is always of me as a person, and of anything which prevents me living the full Christian life. Everything I say or do in the name of Christ is a healing operation. Any over-emphasis on physical, emotional or spiritual healing destroys the unity of my human personality. This book I hope gives a balanced view on Christian healing.

One day I must die, but even death has no victory over me because Jesus my Lord has conquered death, which for me and for every Christian has lost its sting. In a world hungry to see God come alive again in people it is up to you and me to allow ourselves to be healed, so that we may live out the Gospel in our daily lives in freedom, love and peace. Because God the Father loves us we experience in the Christ in each other "His Healing Touch". I pray that this may not be so much a book on healing but a healing book. In that it will have achieved its purpose.

I owe my gratitude in the writing of this book to the many thousands with whom I have experienced healing. It has transformed my life because it has widened my spiritual horizons and deepened my love of God. In all sorts of different ways people have been an inspiration to me in the healing ministry, but none more so than Oonagh Watters whom the Spirit has blessed and anointed in a very special way. She and others in our Community for Inner Healing are a source of strength and encouragement to carry on this very special work of the Gospel. The typing was done by Anne McQuaid, who in the process was healed, together with her family. This book touched her as I pray it will do everyone who reads it and is open to the Spirit.

October 1986   Michael Buckley

1.

What is Healing?

Healing is a very much misunderstood word. To many people it simply means faith healing which cures people physically and emotionally, mainly through the action of someone with special inner powers of healing. Christian healing is not faith healing. Its power rests in the person of Christ who restores us to a full and proper relationship with God the Father, with our neighbour and within ourself.

This threefold restoration of broken relationships we call by the theological name of "reconciliation". It is *the most radical form of healing*. In a sense, every form of reconciliation is a healing, and every healing is a form of reconciliation. The two are inseparably linked together in the mission of Christ and his Church. Just as reconciliation radically restores our relationship with God, our neighbour and ourselves, so *healing gives us the means to live this restored relationship in our daily lives*. Healing is as essential to the Christian life as is reconciliation, just as our continued heartbeat and breathing are necessary for human life. *Christians need both reconciliation and healing*. Remove one or the other and there is no living Gospel left. Christians everywhere accept the word "reconciliation", but many find it difficult to appreciate the true meaning of "healing". It will help to clarify the issue if we describe what we mean by both words.

What is reconciliation? Reconciliation makes us new people. In Christ we are a new creation. We were dead through sin, and God sent his Son to bring us new life:

"And for anyone who is in Christ, there is a new creation; the old creation has gone, and now the new one is here. It is all God's work. It was God who reconciled us to himself through Christ" (2 Corinthians 5:17-18). Reconciliation is the new life of the Spirit by which we are introduced into a new loving relationship with God our Father, from which flow true loving relationships with our neighbour, and a true love of ourselves through the power of the Spirit of Christ which is in us. This threefold relationship spanning the whole spectrum of our lives as persons was disrupted by sin in a way which will be described in the chapter "Disease and Remedy – Sin and Repentance". Christ came to a people who were dead through sin so that by his life, death and resurrection and the sending of the Holy Spirit we might live the new life. That which is broken in man, Christ the reconciler makes whole, that which is empty he fills to overflowing, and that which was destroyed by sin he restores and recreates in a new and more glorious way. His whole life and mission is to reconcile, *to restore broken relationships with God*, so that once again under the influence of the Holy Spirit we can call him "Father". He is *the peace-maker for all mankind* "for he is the peace between us" (Ephesians 2:14), and to all who acknowledge him as Lord there is a new and more fulfilling identity and purpose so that we are *at one within ourselves*. We were created originally in God's image, now we are recreated in the image of Christ, the first-born of all creatures "because God wanted all perfection to be found in him and all things to be reconciled through him and for him" (Colossians 1:18–19). Reconciliation in Christ gives us this wonderful new life of the Spirit.

What is healing? Christian healing frees us from all those elements in our life and world which hinder us from living the new life of reconciliation in our daily lives of Christian pilgrimage. *Reconciliation gives us a new heart; healing* *pumps the blood to every part of our body*. It enters every element of our personality previously diseased by sin, and heals it so that the kingdom of Christ may reign and triumph there. Even though reconciled and called to the new life we still live under the sign of sin. Just as Christ came to reconcile people so his healing extends to the whole person in every situation in which he finds himself. He did not come simply to save our souls or physically restore our twisted physical bodies. Christian healing is not just physical or emotional healing, nor the forgiving of sin, but is all these, and much more. Jesus came to save us as persons. The Hebrews, among whom he ministered in his earthly life, did not think of a person as divided into body and soul, but as a whole person with body, soul, feelings and a personal historical background stretching back in the human family tree. For the Hebrews, to heal a person was to heal them in all that they were. *Christian healing, therefore, involves a person's whole world.*

Called as Christians to live the new life, nevertheless we suffer from the withdrawal symptoms of sin. It is to his Father's glory that we should be fully human, fully alive, and so Christ heals us and our wounded world of everything that prevents us from living the full life of reconciliation and from being whole, human, Christian people. This healing is as much to do with our minds and bodies as with our souls. It involves us in living as full a life as possible in this world because the kingdom has already come on earth, without having to wait "aimlessly" for the world that has yet to come. Healing a person's body is as important as healing a person's soul if the body hinders the person from living the full Christian life, the new life of reconciliation. Time and again I shall return to this proclamation on healing: **Christ wants every aspect of ourselves and our lives to be healed, if without this healing we would not be able to live the new life to the full**. If we believe that we are called to live the new life through reconciliation then we must also equally believe in Christian healing which allows us to do so.

Wherever the Gospel of reconciliation is being preached in today's world there also will be the need for Christian healing. If you deny the latter, then all you have done is erect a petrol station on a mountainside with no means of access, so that it cannot receive regular supplies of petrol or help customers on their journey. *Healing is the outreach of reconciliation*, the most powerful evangelistic weapon in the armoury of committed Christians. It is right therefore that we should concentrate our minds and our hearts on Christian healing, not only to understand and appreciate its effect in our lives, but to use it as a means for furthering Christ's kingdom on earth. "God has entrusted to us the news that they are reconciled. So we are ambassadors for Christ; it is as though God were appealing through us, and the appeal that we make in Christ's name is: be reconciled to God" (2 Corinthians 5:19–20). Through Christian healing the message of reconciliation is heard more clearly and followed more closely. The Kingdom of God becomes more incarnate among us as believers as we are healed or heal through the power of the Holy Spirit. This healing force is at work today in our Church and world so that the love of God the Father, and the living presence of Jesus Christ, may be made manifest in our lives. I do not want to be told about salvation by some "evangelist" mouthing for the umpteenth time that "God loves me". I want to *see* that healing love in action in people's lives and in my own. *I want to see salvation in healing*. It happened in Christ's time on earth. Why shouldn't it happen today?

I believe that Jesus Christ reconciles people today and that he heals in our lives and world. He healed in his own lifetime on earth and reconciled people to his Father. His healing was necessary then for his Gospel of reconciliation, so that his followers might live the new life he came to establish. It is just as necessary today, and yet there are Christians who do not accept Christian healing as part of Christ's and the Church's mission today. They think that the "well of healing" dried up with the Early Church. How wrong they are! Our Church and world need healing today just as much as, if not more so than, when Christ healed so stupendously in Galilee two thousand years ago. You can be reconciled to God the Father and be a "born again" Christian who calls Jesus your "Lord", and yet you still need to be healed throughout your life because of your "wounded self and world". "I cannot understand my own behaviour", writes St Paul. "I fail to carry out the things I want to do, and I find myself doing the very things I hate . . . The fact is, I know of nothing good living in me – living, that is, in my unspiritual self – for though the will to do what is good is in me, the performance is not, with the result that instead of doing the good things I want to do, I carry out the sinful things I do not want. When I act against my will, then, it is not my true self doing it, but sin which lives in me" (Romans 7:15,18–20). St Paul was a "born again" Christian who acknowledged his need of healing. The "born again" Christians, or the totally institutionalized church people, who claim to be so "reconciled", so saved, as not to need further healing, live lives that in my opinion do not ring true to the full Christian Gospel of healing *and* reconciliation. The fact that we have been reconciled does not mean that we will not fall from grace in the future. Christians of all shades of belief *always* need healing. To pretend the opposite is a sign of spiritual arrogance and self-righteousness.

If we limit the healing ministry of Christ to his three short years on earth, and the life of the Early Church, then we are limiting the ministry of his Church, his presence and his power within it. Reconciliation and healing are essential to the Church's mission today as a living sign of Christ, "for where two or three meet in my name, I shall be there with them" (Matthew 18:20). Christ makes himself present in his Church through reconciliation *and* healing. The promise of his healing power to his followers extends to all those who believe in him: "I tell you most solemnly, whoever believes in me will perform the same works as I do myself, he will do even greater works" (John 14:12). Christ heals today through you and me and all those who believe in his name.

Because he is true to his promises, the extent of his healing power at work in us is only hindered by our lack of faith. If only we believed, if only! Surely Christian healing is the greatest proof of Christ's divine presence among us. He told the followers of John the Baptist "Go back and tell John what you hear and see; the blind see again, and the lame walk, lepers are cleansed, and the deaf hear, and the dead are raised to life and the Good News is proclaimed to the poor; and happy is the man who does not lose faith in me" (Matthew 11:4–6). Jesus used his healing power to proclaim reconciliation "that the Kingdom of God has overtaken you" (Matthew 12:28) when he healed the blind and dumb demoniac "so that the dumb man could speak and see" (Matthew 12:22). If Christ used healing as a sign of his mission of reconciliation then so should we in the Church.

Unless, and until, we give Christian healing its proper place in the life and ministry of the Church today, then evangelization will be a very muted voice, and Christians will limp their way through a crippled existence bereft of much of the juice and joy of Christian living. When healing is at the forefront of ministry then Christ will become the centre of the circle of God's love and ours, as he gives pattern and direction to the love-exchange. He will become the dialysis machine which purifies our blood of its poisonous waste residue of sin. He will liberate us from the prison of self, and lead us on the glorious way to the Father as freed children who truly love him.

Christ heals us as persons from all those things which hold us back from living the new life of reconciliation. Those illnesses may be of the

(a) **Soul**—he heals by forgiving us our sins, so enabling us to allow that forgiveness to flow out to others, and not least of all to ourselves.
(b) **Emotions**—he heals by mending hurtful memories or anxiety caused by stress, irrational guilt, fear and all those psychological upsets which disturb our peace of mind and soul.
(c) **Body**—illnesses caused by physical diseases or defects which hinder us from the loving service of God our Father and our neighbour.

While there are priorities in healing, nevertheless, *all healing* however intensely physical *is related to the whole person and to reconciliation*, and therefore has emotional and spiritual overtones which affect the soul and emotions of the healed person. Because healing affects the whole person, then the spiritual, emotional and physical healings are interactive.

Let me give you an example. I met Joe some years ago at a prayer meeting, to which he was reluctantly dragged by his wife. He was very bitter because the severe rheumatoid arthritis in his hands drastically limited his work as an architect. As usual in these cases, when we had prayed for some time together as a group I was led by the Spirit to take Joe into a private room because I discerned that the root cause of his disorder was much deeper. I told him his sins were forgiven, at which point he broke down, saying that he felt God no longer loved him because of some hidden sins of his past of which he had not repented. He went on to tell me of his very poor relationship with his wife and two teenage children. We traced this to his insecurity in business due to his jealousy of his partner, who seemed to be more in demand with their clients. Things reached such a climax that he purchased a gun and bullets, with which he intended to kill his wife and children, his partner and then himself. He confessed this to his family, and their reunion was one of the most healing events I have ever been privileged to witness. I then asked him to write a letter of reconciliation to his partner. He had not been able to hold a pen for over a year, but at my request he sat down and wrote a letter in which he asked forgiveness for all the trouble he had caused, and as he wrote his hand visibly changed, becoming as normal as it was before the onset of his physical affliction. Today his family are among the happiest I know. His business is prospering, and he is the leader of a flourishing prayer group. Joe was healed as a person in his soul, his emotions and his body.

As I repeatedly stress in this book Christian healing does not divide the human person into compartments of soul, emotions and body. They are integral parts of the whole person, and to heal one aspect is to affect the others. To the extent that any institutional church or group limits the healing power of Christ to one aspect, e.g. physical healing, to the exclusion of the others, then it is to that extent less Christian, and less true to the Gospel it claims it is commissioned to proclaim.

Some churches which are so insistent on reconciliation and on their power to forgive sins in Jesus' name, nevertheless look with suspicion, even with condemnation, on any of their members who would dare to exercise the ministry of physical and emotional healing. Surely the claim for the "greater" healing of sin must presuppose the power of the "lesser" physical and emotional healings?

Many powerful institutional churches have assumed into their system of thinking and believing the Greek philosophical concept of the dichotomy of soul and body, and a theology which presumes that Jesus came to save souls not bodies. Many evangelical and Pentecostal churches, on the other hand, highlight physical healing as "the main platform" of their ministry, and interrelate bodily defects with personal sin. These churches never have any pretensions to claiming that they have been given the power to forgive sins in Jesus' name. In fact the two forms of healing are closely interrelated, as is shown by the story of the paralytic whose sins were forgiven first by Jesus, before any physical healing took place (Mark 2:3–12). The limitation of Christ's healing power in any aspect of human life shows up a false philosophy of the nature of the human person, as well as a narrow theological concept of sin, and a thorough lack of appreciation of how God the Father's love overcomes all sin in Jesus Christ his Son. *It is the* person *who is sick in soul, body and emotions so that he cannot live the new life, and it is the* person *that Christ always heals.* We seem to presume always that a person suffering some physical or deep emotional illness is not thereby correspondingly affected in his spiritual life and his relationship with God his Father. I have witnessed hundreds of people who have been liberated within themselves to praise God in freedom and joy because they have been healed physically or emotionally. There are deep-rooted antipathies to such healings, which in turn need healing if the churches are to fulfil their role in Christian healing and reconciliation. Is it because there is a lack of faith in many Christians that so relatively few are engaged in the healing ministry?

There are no limits to Christian healing and reconciliation on the part of God our loving father. He wants us to be whole and healthy, to praise, glorify and serve him freely and lovingly. It is we who have put the limits on Christian healing because of our lack of faith and courage to step out in his healing name. There are many people crippled today in our churches, bowed down by insupportable burdens of soul, mind and body, with no one to heal them in Christ's name, to enable and encourage them to live the new life of reconciliation. The Church's identity will become clearer, its message more powerful, when it follows the example of its Master. "That evening, after sunset, they brought to him all who were sick and those who were possessed by devils. The whole town came crowding round the door, and he cured many who were suffering from diseases of one kind or another" (Mark 1:32–34).

2.

I Believe in Healing

I believe in Christian healing. Throughout my life I have been healed as a person at many levels: physical, emotional and spiritual. Healing for me is a personal experience. This healing process has gone on all through my life, is still going on and will not end until the day I die. I know that I shall never be able to say that I am so completely healed within myself that I shall never need healing again. In fact the opposite is true. As I grow older and become more accustomed to healing, I find that when I am healed of one thing I then need healing from another, not only because I live in a world which is hostile and unhealthy to the Christian – "The whole world lies in the power of the Evil One . . ." (1 John 5:19) but because of the effects of sin within myself, which leave me a wounded person.

Like every person who is engaged in the ministry of healing I regard myself as a "wounded healer". The Old and New Testaments proclaim the loving goodness of God as a Father, but more than anything else it is when I am touched by His healing power that I realize more fully and personally that God is my Father, who wants me to be a healthy, happy and wholesome person. The healing power of the Bible comes alive in my life. The word of God is living and active, and when it touches my life I experience its healing power and know, as well as believe, that God is a healing Father.

Healing is so personal and experiential that it is well nigh impossible even to describe it to someone who has not had a similar experience. This is one of the reasons, I suppose, why healing is so suspect in the traditional churches, and is commonly regarded as unacademic and emotional. It cannot be analysed, synthesized or "learned". We know we have been healed but we cannot explain in spiritual, medical or psychological terms exactly what happened and why. We can only give the reply of the man born blind whom Jesus healed on the Sabbath day. When the Jews asked him, "What did he do to you? How did he open your eyes?" he replied, "I only know that I was blind and now I can see" (John 9:25-26).

If you are sceptical or cynical about healing then this book has nothing to offer you, except to suggest that you read the Gospel of Jesus Christ with the thought before you that perhaps the events recorded there were not of a bygone age with no power or relevance to the world in which we live, and that maybe healing is still present among us as a visible sign of God the Father's enduring love and power. If this were not so then the gospels would just be historical books, and the healing Christ would not be alive and active today in our Church and world. Yet the Gospel is not just a set of historical books but the healing word of God alive in our world now.

The healing power of God is still active today and I bear testimony to it in my own life. I wish to record in this book just three personal healings, even though there have been many others much more spectacular than these three simple ones. If you do not believe in these then what of the others I could have chosen!

My first healing was **physical**. When I was just five years old I came home in the evening from a party given by one of my classmates. I proceeded to get violently sick, and after about an hour my mother sent for the family doctor, Tom Blake, who was concerned because I began to lose consciousness. My father wrapped me in a blanket and carried me the few hundred yards from our home to the nearest hospital, run by the Mercy Sisters in Cork. That night I lapsed into a coma and two other doctors were summoned for their opinion. Both Dr Kearney and Dr Halley, highly respected members of their profession, said I was suffering from an acute form of food poisoning, and there was nothing anyone could do for me. I was fed intravenously and, medicine not being as advanced then as it is today, I still carry the marks on my body where the tubes were inserted into my chest and legs. I lay there for six days in a comatose state, with my face, I am told, a deathly purple colour. Subconsciously I heard the comings and goings of my family and the quiet sobbing of my parents, who never seemed to leave my bedside. It was an eerie experience as if I were a spectator, a stranger watching everything that was happening to me. Every so often two Sisters of Mercy would come into the room and say prayers at my bedside. After that I heard occasional hushed voices coming from the corner of the room. It was like being at my own "wake".

On the sixth day after my admission to the hospital, Sister Raymond, the matron, came into the room, unfastened the intravenous tubes, wrapped me in a blanket and brought me and my parents to the convent chapel. She laid me on the altar and offered my life to the Lord, praying that I would live to do great things for Him. She spoke to God personally, as if she knew him as a friend. I can still hear her voice. How I heard it first, when I was comatose, I shall never know. It was redolent with faith and confidence that God would restore me well and healthy to my parents. Later that morning I remember opening my eyes, and holding my hands out to my mother and asking for something to drink. There was a joy in that hospital room which I have experienced time and again whenever God heals his people. Within three days I was back at home with my parents, who never ceased to remind me of what happened through God's loving care and why I should always be grateful to him.

Years later, as a priest, I returned to the Mercy Hospital and asked Sister Raymond how and why she did it. The answer was simple and direct. "I felt sorry for your parents, I thought it a shame to see such a young child dying, so I just asked God to heal you, and he did." She had never read a book on healing, never been to Lourdes, was not a charismatic and was as traditional a Catholic as one would ever find in Ireland. I believe God used her to be an instrument of my physical healing in a situation where three doctors had given up all medical hope for my survival. I am alive today because of Sister Raymond's prayer to a loving God who had compassion on sorrowing parents. I believe also that my physical healing was related to my spiritual life. The one leads to the other, and in my experience this is always so with physical healing. God heals more than the body, and whenever he physically heals it is for a deeper, spiritual reason. In fact no healing of any kind takes place without affecting every part of our human personality and our relationship with God, our neighbour and ourselves. In later life I prayed to him for physical protection in my work for peace and reconciliation in Northern Ireland, and he rescued me time and time again from the most hair-raisingly dangerous situations. It was a repetition of Daniel in the lion's den. I gave my life to God in working for peace and reconciliation, and wherever I go and in whatever situation I find myself I completely trust my physical safety to him. I am at peace always, not because I am brave, but because I trust that the Lord will deliver me safe and sound.

So much for physical healing, to which I shall devote a complete chapter later in the book. The second healing in my life concerns **inner healing**, or healing of memories. For many years two objectives have dominated my life and prayers as a priest, namely peace and reconciliation in Northern Ireland, and true Christian renewal and evangelization in the Church. You would have expected that all church-goers would have rallied to both causes, but I soon discovered that this sadly was not so. Peace in Ireland had its price which few were prepared to pay, and renewal in the Church meant change, radical at times. Attitudes to my work, and what I stood for, ranged from apathy to hostility. It was a hurt that was hard to bear.

For years I suffered from this deep hurt inflicted on me by a church which I loved so well, and which was so much a part of me. I talked it over endlessly with friends, but I could not come to terms with it in my spiritual life. Prayers became a series of angry questions to God – "Why do they not understand what I am trying to do?" I prayed for deliverance from the hurt which was gnawing away at my soul like a cancer. I was dying inside. I wanted to be free of the hurt and soar above it like an eagle, but I remained a budgie in my cage singing about my own little hurt. One day in my study, when I returned from Northern Ireland where I had been at the scene of another outrageous killing, I realized what was happening to me, and how damaged I was in my memory and in my attitude to God. I fell on my knees, or rather I was forced on to them, and asked God to deliver me and give me deep inner peace. Within seconds the burden was lifted. I shall never forget that moment when the deep inner peace of Christ flooded my soul and every part of my body. It was as if I were lifted up above the situation, and could see it all not so much from the vantage point of a cross but from the hill of the resurrection. I was free, gloriously free, from hurtful memories, free to live the full Christian life in a peace which no one or nothing would take away from me again. Not only my prayer life but my whole life changed. I never lost that sense of deep inner peace again.

Through the sense of deep hurt I experienced and the feeling of rejection by those who should have been my friends and co-workers, I was spiritually healed of seeking human respect and approval of everything I do. The loneliness of six years without any diocesan work, and being a non-person, the loss of the Pastoral and Ecumenical Centre which I had seen grow so rapidly in prophecy and achievement over a decade, were as nothing compared to the healing I experienced at the Lord's hands. Through this healing of memories of rejection I have learned to grapple with human fear in the face of physical and psychological violence on many other occasions, with the full assurance that I believed I was doing what God wanted me to do. I could not be anywhere else, or do anything else, and live at peace with my Christian conscience, because no matter what anyone said or thought I had to be God's man. Institutions and people took their proper place on the rungs of the ladder of my spiritual priorities. From my healing onwards God the Father, and Christ the Lord, became and remain the only supreme and absolute in my life. Through that inner healing of memories I have truly learned at least some of the meaning of the First Commandment, "You shall have no gods except me". In the inner healing I lost nothing but my hurt, and my whole spiritual life changed in a way that would not have been possible without both the hurt and the healing. In a strange way, which I cannot explain except to those who have had a similar experience, I am grateful for the hurt. It uprooted me and at the same time planted me in a whole new way of life and thinking. God, love and life became a new language. So much for physical and emotional or inner healing.

The third incident of healing in my life concerns my need for **repentance for my sins**. Like everyone else born into this world, I was a sinner not only because I am heir to

Adam's sin, but especially because of my own personal sins. This required the healing of my soul if I were to live a full, healthy Christian life. The deepest form of healing will always be the forgiveness of sin, the putting right of our relationship with God. There is a sense in which every other form of healing is related to this, but the tendency will always remain for would-be healers to oversimplify healing and reduce to sin every form of illness, physical or emotional, whether of oneself, one's parents or family tree. My big personal sin was that for years I did not know, love or serve God as a Father – and how destructive of Christian spirituality this way of thinking is.

Right into my adult life I looked upon him as a judge who would punish me severely for my tiniest fault, rather than as a Father who loved me as his very own child. Fear not love, sin not grace, life not death, dominated my spiritual consciousness. "Think of the love that the Father has lavished on us, by letting us be called God's children; and that is what we are" (1 John 3:1). Religion was learned by rote from my teachers, so that I had all the answers to questions nobody asked, least of all myself. God was never real for me at school, even though I always seemed to get the prize for religious education!

I did not really know God the Father as a person. In a sense I could identify with Christ and felt sorry for the way he was treated, not only by the Jews and the Roman soldiers, but by his own Father who allowed him to suffer in such a terrible way. If God could do this to his own Son who was sinless, then what would he do to me who was full of sin!! I felt that deep down I was an awful person hidden from the world by a mask. I was literally terrified of hell, about which I had had many nightmares. If I did wrong then I was afraid that a car would knock me down in the street, or that I would fall through a manhole! God was not my Father by any stretch of the imagination. He was watching me to catch me out! So I concentrated on Christ, and pushed the Fatherhood of God to the periphery of my spiritual life. When I came to stand before the judgement seat of God I hoped that Christ would speak for me and protect me from his Father's just anger.

Over the years this very wrong way of spiritual thinking has changed for me. It was a gradual process rather than an immediate healing – no Damascus story here. Unlike the healing of memories which I can relate to a definite time and place, the healing of my soul came gradually through people and events. They were instruments of the Holy Spirit. If Christian people were really honest they would admit that the full awareness of the power of the Holy Spirit does not as a rule come in a blinding flash, even though we can become aware of it instantly as if we never knew it before. We do know, through various graces of people and events, but not in this particular, compelling, Damascus way. The graces in my life all helped to clear the spiritual blockage which prevented God getting through to me as a Father, but the final spiritual healing in me came about ultimately by the unique power of the Holy Spirit. "Everyone moved by the Spirit is a son of God. The spirit you received is not the spirit of slaves bringing fear into your lives again; it is the spirit of sons, and it makes us cry out, 'Abba, Father!' The Spirit himself and our spirit bear united witness that we are children of God. And if we are children we are heirs as well: heirs of God and coheirs with Christ, sharing his sufferings so as to share his glory" (Romans 8:14-17).

Through this spiritual healing God became a reality for me, and set me off on a completely new way of thinking and acting. For the first time I allowed God fully to be the Father of my life, and it is incredible how this has changed everything. I know now that no one can be a Christian unless he truly believes that God is his Father and Christ is his Lord. I could have studied all the books on religion and endured the most crippling physical hardships, but until I was released by the Spirit to love and serve God freely, my faith or life did not come truly and fully alive. I thought I knew God until then but I didn't really, at least not in a fully loving way. The Spirit set me, a prisoner, free, and this is the Christian Gospel I shall proclaim without let or hindrance until he calls me home. Being once healed I felt called more and more to the ministry of healing.

Before the Spirit released me, my fear of God diminished gradually over the years, but until the Spirit came it was still the wrong kind of fear. Now my fear is not the *servile* fear of a guilty servant who fears his master's wrath, but the loving or *filial* fear of a son who wants above everything else in his life to do whatever the Father wants. Obedience is of the essence of Christian healing. The Spirit is teaching me how to love God, my neighbour and myself in the way God wants me to, and the deepening of my capacity to love, like love itself, will never come to an end. My healing is a continuing, never-ending process. I believe he can do anything with and for me, because he has done so much already. That is why healing is part and parcel of my life, mission and destiny. I find the Christian life more exciting now, with both its bumps and bonuses. It is certainly never dull. At this late stage I think I am beginning to understand my life, and God's, a little better.

3.

Disease and Remedy – Sin and Repentance

Why do we all need reconciliation and healing? The answer quite simply is that we are diseased, not at ease, within ourselves, with our neighbour or with God. Scarcely had the human race begun when an alien force invaded our lives and world, affecting us all: that alien force we call "sin". To the unbeliever the world has always been as it is today, with its unrelenting struggle for power and survival. To talk of anything different, such as the healing power of a loving God, who really cares for us and wants us healthy, is like telling an isolated leper colony that there are people who are not lepers, or that they can be helped by medical aid when they have never encountered a doctor or nurse, or even heard of medicine: they are lepers and lepers they will remain; there never was, or ever could be, another plan or way of life for them. This is their conditioned way of thinking and acting.

In our sick world there are few who think of healing. Fatalism too has gripped the minds and hearts of many Christians who have abandoned the practice and even the hope of healing. Religion has become for them an escape route, an opt-out from reality, an opium to drug the pain of inevitable suffering and lack of fulfilment in their lives. We need encouragement from the institutional churches to believe that God is a loving Father who wants us whole, and therefore heals us. Yet it often takes more faith inside than outside the institutional churches to believe in healing, reconciliation and the fullness of life in this world as well as the next! They tell us that we live in a vale of tears, and that "suffering is the badge of all our tribe" so we just have to "grin and bear it". We are told to regard ourselves with low esteem, and instead of reflecting the brightness of God who made us "a little less than the angels" we fear that deep inside us there lurks the animal, with its insatiable appetite for self-destruction. Fear, not love, rules our lives.

Yet the Good News was meant to set us free of fear and free to love, and to make us into a person transformed from a slave into a son. We were to be "whole" people again. The ideal Christian is a person who lives at peace within himself because his life is saturated by the healing oil of the Gospel, which uplifts him so that his very life bears witness to its intrinsic power. He is made and re-created in the image of God. He is meant to make the Gospel his way of life, but we have only to look inside ourselves to realize that this is not so. We fall short in practice. The seeds of weakness within us in the family tree go back to the very origin of man. This is the root cause of our disease and our need for reconciliation and healing. It will help us in our understanding of reconciliation and healing to recapitulate briefly the history of the "fall and rise" of man.

The Fall and Rise of Man

The first two chapters of Genesis clearly spell out God's love and purpose for the human race and world. His creation was an act of love, and the peak of his creation was man and woman: "God created man in the image of himself, in the image of God he created him, male and female, he created them" (Genesis 1:27). God loved his creation and his living creatures, especially man and woman, whom he made in his own likeness. He wanted his first human beings to be healthy, and that is why God blessed them, saying to them, "Be fruitful and multiply, fill the earth and conquer it. Be masters of the fish of the sea, the birds of heaven, and all living animals on the earth. God saw all that he had made and indeed it was very good" (Genesis 28:31). The true purpose of creation was, and is, wholeness. Everything on earth was ordered in the beginning, each in its own place, and man was the priest of creation ordained to praise God, to love him and to serve him in perfect freedom. When we look around us in the world, we know that this plan went horrendously wrong. Modern man, with his insatiable passion for conflict and the destruction of his own species, can hardly be said to reflect the real image of God. The peace and happiness of the Garden of Eden seem a myth, a fantasy, and our chaotic world the only reality. The Bible tells us that God is not a monster who spawns countless little monsters. He does not want us to be deformed, spiritually, morally or physically. What went wrong with God's plan for our health and wholeness?

God created man free, and to be human man had to remain free. This was his unique gift from God. Freedom gave man the wonderful opportunity of freedom of choice, a gift that no other living creature possessed, and in this freedom he came closest to the nature of God himself. While all other creatures obeyed their instincts, man alone would choose, by the use of his intellect and will, to do what he wanted. So while the rest of creation obeyed, *man through sin disobeyed*. He said to his Creator, "I will not obey you", and through his disobedience the priest of creation turned upside down the world God left him. "Sin entered the world through one man, and through sin death, and thus death has spread through the whole human race because everyone has sinned" (Romans 5:12). So our human nature became diseased, ill at ease within itself, because falling into the temptation to be "like Gods" (Genesis 3:5) man frustrated creation to such an extent "that it was made unable to attain its purpose" (Romans 8:20) and was wounded, being "red in tooth and claw". However, "it still retains the hope of being freed from its slavery to decadence, to enjoy the same freedom and glory as the children of God" (Romans 8:21).

Sin, which in its essence is man deciding to become the sole master of his own destiny, destroys the true relationship of love and obedience between himself and God, sets brother against brother in the human family, and destroys the wholeness of man as a person, leaving him at war within himself. Inner peace was lost to the human race long before Cain slew Abel. It is towards recovering and maintaining this true relationship with God, our neighbour and ourselves that all Christian reconciliation and healing are directed.

The Effects of Sin

Through sin man is *alienated* from:

    A. God his loving Father.
    B. The human community.
    C. His true self.

He needs to be *reconciled* through:

    A. Conversion to God in repentance.
    B. A return to God's people.
    C. The integration of his true self.

The human race by its own unaided efforts could not effect this reconciliation, and so God the Father, in love for his human family, while it was like the Prodigal Son, still a "long way off", went out to meet it in love, through his only Son. The coming of Jesus into human history meant that God, in the person of his Son through the Incarnation, took upon himself our sin-laden human race.

> His state was divine,
> yet he did not cling
> to his equality with God
> but emptied himself
> to assume the condition of a slave,
> and became as men are (Philippians 2:6-7).

Though himself personally sinless, as man the innocent Lamb of God had to live out his divine Sonship identifying himself with our alienation. "For our sake God made the sinless one into sin, so that in him we might become the goodness of God" (2 Corinthians 5:12).

Christ's life was the epitome of loving *obedience* to his heavenly Father. He obeyed as the human race should have done from the beginning of its existence. This obedience involved Christ in the laying down of his life out of love for his Father and for us: "A man can have no greater love than to lay down his life for his friends" (John 15:13). It was his Father's will that perfect Sonship should reveal itself in perfect obedience, and that the death of his only Son would demonstrate that the love of God the Father is greater than man's sinfulness!

> God loved the world so much
> that he gave his only Son,
> so that everyone who believes in him may not be lost
> but may have eternal life (John 3:16).

The Son's testimony of total self-giving in obedience draws forth from the Father his testimony to his Son. The humiliated Servant is enthroned as the Lord of Glory and is revealed as the Christ, the only Son of God, who died and rose again for our sakes. In his death, resurrection, ascension and sending of the Holy Spirit he is our reconciliation and our hope.

> God raised him high
> and gave him the name
> which is above all other names
> so that all beings
> in the heavens, on earth and in the underworld,
> should bend the knee at the name of Jesus
> and that every tongue should acclaim
> Jesus Christ as Lord,
> to the glory of God, the Father
> (Philippians 2:9–11).

In the risen, ascended Christ, a new age is inaugurated. Man is reconciled to God the Father, the human community and his true self. Yet *in this new age of reconciliation there remain post-operational adhesions which need healing.* The twin powers of reconciliation and healing are at work all through our lives as Christians, so that we may persevere in the good life until Christ will come again at the final consummation of everything. It will help us in our efforts to understand Christian healing if we dwell a little longer on the three main areas of sin and repentance.

Alienation from, and Conversion to, God our Loving Father

The refusal of Adam to obey God strikes a chord in our hearts, especially in times of physical or mental suffering or spiritual dryness. Even though we are Christians the call of the "selfish-self" is very strong. I have repeatedly been told that "born again" Christians should not feel that way, but one has only to read St Paul, the prototype of "born again" Christians, to know that is not so. The old Adam lives on in all of us, however fervent and traumatic our Christian conversion may have been. Personally I do not find it easy to obey God in every situation, but I would rather make a poor attempt at this Christian ideal than slavishly conform to purely human rules which bring a sense of "social security" and deaden the still, small voice of conscience. Yet the reluctance to obey God in matters that entail sacrifice has a siren attraction which gives us the illusion of independence over our own destiny. Like the Prodigal Son we demand in advance our share of the inheritance, and live the "good life" far away from God and our Christian roots (Luke 15:11-32). This life soon becomes a nightmare, and we feel alienated from God our Father on whom we have turned our backs. Realizing what we have done, we receive the grace of repentance, and being truly sorry for betraying a Father's love we return to ask for his forgiveness and mercy. The act of reconciliation is complete, and yet there will still come times in the future when we need healing. Let me give you an example.

Tim was the son of a wealthy Dublin industrialist. For years after completing his university degree he led a debauched life, with drugs, drink and women. He was constantly in debt due to gambling, and his father unfailingly bailed him out. One day he had a very serious car accident, in which he nearly died. It had a traumatic effect on him and his life did a complete "U" turn. He settled down, became an excellent, caring son, married a first-class Catholic and was in every sense of the word a Christian. Yet there were times when the shadows of the past came back to draw a heavy veil over the glory and face of Christ, and the initial warmth of Christian belonging felt the chill wind of remorse. Tim needed healing and came to me time and again that I might minister to him. In his case, as in many others, after the initial reconciliation and repentance, there was need for healing of his soul. This is another example of reconciliation and healing being two sides of the same coin which purchased wholeness for Tim. I have found in healing that this feeling of guilt over the past, and the growing awareness of the wrong things they have done, increase the sense of guilt in people, to the point where they "feel" that God cannot forgive them completely. They still believe that God is their loving Father but inner peace is far away. It is for such as these that the inner healing of memories is so vital as a follow-up to reconciliation.

Alienation in the Human Community

This is a consequence of the disorder of sin in our lives. Every sin, either directly or indirectly, harms the community, because being people wounded by sin we seek our own interests first, to the neglect of others. There is no need to stress this disorder because we have ample evidence to prove it, not only when we look around us but especially when we examine our own lives and interests as well. Our minds and hearts are disorientated, so that our priorities are upside down, and life in the world of human relations becomes a battle for survival. The great need in our world today is the healing of human relationships in every aspect of society. We have to learn to forgive our enemies from deep within us, if we are to find true peace of mind and forgiveness for our souls. This spiritual healing is necessary for our survival and growth as Christians. An example will help to illustrate this.

In Seymour Hill, Belfast, during the height of the conflict between the two communities when feelings were running high, I led a service of healing and forgiveness. I was interrupted as soon as I began by Betty, a Protestant woman, who told me in bitter tones and words that she hated all Catholics. When I asked why, she pointed to a woman in the congregation and said, "Because her son killed my son, and since then I have not had a moment's peace in my mind and heart. I cannot even say a prayer." Kathleen, the Catholic woman, replied equally bitterly and strongly – "and my son is in prison for life for that killing, which was caused by all the injustices heaped upon us Catholics over the years. I can't pray either because my heart is full of bitterness and pain." The atmosphere was electric and summed up for me all the tension and bitterness in Northern Ireland between the two communities. We prayed deeply for reconciliation and healing, and eventually Betty and Kathleen embraced each other in mutual sorrow, forgiveness and reconciliation. It will stay with me to the end of my life. Both women still need healing from time to time, when the mists of the pain of loss torment the mothers' minds and hearts. How true it is that "Christ is the peace between us" (Ephesians 2:4), and if we do not forgive those who trespass against us then the healing love of God will not flow into our lives, nor will he use us to heal others. "The amount you measure out is the amount you will be given back" (Luke 6:38). God's forgiving love in the community never flows through a blocked pipe. Healing unblocks the pipe of hurt, painful memories, bitterness and revenge.

The Integration of Man's True Self

Just as sin gradually corrupts and fragments the human person, so, as a general rule, repentance gradually purifies and integrates him. It will involve him in a whole change of life and attitude, in which the love of God and of his neighbour must come before love of self. This requires an on-going healing process. The deepening awareness of

God's love as a Father leads to a deepening awareness of sin. To minimize the battle within the soul and mind of the repentant sinner, and to pretend that once he has given his life to Christ then the turmoil within him is finished, is something I have *never* encountered in over thirty years' ministry. To pretend otherwise because he has received the grace of reconciliation does untold damage to truth, reality and the gospel message. Even if you have a "road to Damascus" experience you still need healing. St Paul needed healing from his physical blindness. We all need healing every day, in case we slip back to our bad old ways. I could give you countless examples but shall take one simple case.

Jane was heavily involved in a physical relationship which she found hard to break. Eventually she wrote to Bernard and told him the affair was over, when she realized that it was coming between herself and God, and did not want to live a double life. For months afterwards she felt the compulsion to ring him and renew the relationship, but on each occasion she was helped by the healing love of the Spirit. The struggle was hard, the price was high, but the peace of soul that followed was worth it all. "I grew as a person", she wrote to me, "and I found a new, deeper respect for myself. God is still very close. He has to be to take my hand because I still feel very shaky and unsure of myself that I will slip back into the old ways."

Sin disturbs us and will go on disturbing us. Even though we know God is our Father, and we are reconciled to him, the attraction to return to the ways of the world still remains. We will never so conquer the world in ourselves that we do not need further healing. In every case where I minister healing, I always pray first for repentance and inner healing of memories before I pray for anything else. I believe inner healing of peace of soul and mind is a very special ministry, to which more and more Christians are being called. Of course I pray also for physical healing, and the Father has answered my prayers in the most wonderful ways, but I still believe that until we face up to sin and its crippling effect on our lives then our healing ministry will be drastically limited. The most difficult healing is of "saved Christians" who feel that they are above healing. If anyone thinks he is so reconciled with God that he does not need further healing because he is saved, then I refer him to St Paul, "For we must be content to hope that we shall be saved – our salvation is not in sight, we should not have to be hoping for it if it were – but, as I say, we must hope to be saved since we are not saved yet – it is something we must wait for with patience" (Romans 8:24-25).

The most profound healing Jesus brought to people in his earthly ministry was not physical healing but the forgiveness of their sins, the classic example of the "priority" of forgiveness of sin over physical healing being recounted in the gospel story of the cure of the paralytic.

Some people came bringing him [Jesus] a paralytic carried by four men, but as the crowd made it impossible to get the man to him, they stripped the roof over the place where Jesus was; and when they had made an opening, they lowered the stretcher on which the paralytic lay. Seeing their faith, Jesus said to the paralytic, "My child, your sins are forgiven". Now some scribes were sitting there, and they thought to themselves, "How can this man talk like that? He is blaspheming. Who can forgive sins but God?" Jesus, inwardly aware that this was what they were thinking, said to them, "Why do you have those thoughts in your hearts? Which of these is easier: to say to the paralytic, 'Your sins are forgiven' or to say, 'Get up, pick up your stretcher and walk?' But to prove to you that the Son of Man has authority on earth to forgive sins" – he said to

42

the paralytic — "I order you: get up, pick up your stretcher, and go off home." And the man got up, picked up his stretcher at once and walked out in front of everyone, so that they were all astounded and praised God saying, "We have never seen anything like this" (Mark 2:3-12).

Sin is the key to the disease in ourselves and our world. We have to proclaim the forgiveness of God our loving Father, revealed in his Son, Jesus Christ:

> The blood of Jesus, his Son
> purifies us from all sin.
> If we say we have no sin in us,
> we are deceiving ourselves
> and refusing to admit the truth;
> but if we acknowledge our sins,
> then God who is faithful and just
> will forgive our sins and purify us
> from everything that is wrong. . . .
> Jesus Christ . . . is the sacrifice
> that takes our sins away,
> and not only ours,
> but the whole world's (1 John 1:7-9, 2:2).

In sorrow we return to our Father's house, where he will nourish and protect us with his healing power. Peace with God through the forgiveness of our sins is the source of our inner peace within ourselves and with our neighbour. In this lies the origin of every form of healing and wholeness.

Healing and reconciliation go on all through our lives until we are finally made whole in heaven. The two saving elements in our Christian lives are often scarcely distinguishable, because it is difficult to delineate where one begins and the other ends. They are both constantly at work interacting in us, so that as we heal in Christ's power and name, we become like him, "wounded healers". Ultimately it is by his wounds that we are reconciled and healed.

4.

The Father Who Wants to Heal Us

If you love someone you want what is best for them. If they are ill then you want them well. How many times have our mothers "kissed better" the bumps and bruises of our childhood! In the same way I believe that God our Father wants to heal us because he loves us in the most special way possible. We cannot rationalize, fully understand or deserve that love, since it is greater than any human love of a parent.

> Does a woman forget her baby at the breast,
> or fail to cherish the son of her womb?
> Yet even if these forget,
> I will never forget you (Isaiah 49:15).

> I myself taught Ephraim to walk,
> I took them in my arms;
> yet they have not understood
> that I was the one looking after them.
> I led them with reins of kindness,
> with leading-strings of love.
> I was like someone who lifts an infant close
> against his cheek;
> stooping down to him I gave him his food
> (Hosea 11:3-4).

One of the great obstacles to healing is the feeling that we deserve to be punished because we do not really love God as we should and do not merit his love. Yet God the Father's love is completely gratuitous. We can never merit it by our own unaided efforts. "Think of the love that the Father has lavished on us, by letting us be called God's children; and that is what we are" (1 John 3:1). Since we are God's children then as a Father he wants us whole and happy, and if we are not then he wants to heal us.

We have tended to forget the all-embracing, healing love of God the Father in our ministry of healing, and have seen it as a kind of divine love that does not penetrate our ordinary world and lives. We have played down Christ's revelation of his Father as someone who sent him to bring us healing. Why? After all, it is his Father's will that we are made whole. We emphasize instead, however subconsciously, the pagan notion of a god who sends suffering as a punishment for our sins, so that Christ becomes his Father's, and our, scapegoat. Why? We have come to look on suffering as a means of "meriting" or "gaining" the Father's love, as if he did not love us already, for who we are. Why do we do this when we are part of his loved creation? It is because it is sin not grace, death not life, fear not love which dominate our religious thinking.

The key to all forms of the ministry of healing lies in our firm belief and total conviction that healing is part of the *ordinary* will of a totally loving Father. Healing of any other kind is limited and limiting. It is not extraordinary that we should be healed. Because God is our Father, he wants us whole while respecting our freedom. The essential Gospel of Christ is that he was sent by the Father to do the Father's will, which was to heal a broken world.

He [God the Father] has sent me to bring the good news to the poor, to proclaim liberty to captives and to the blind new sight, to set the downtrodden free, to proclaim the Lord's year of favour (Luke 4:18).

Christ proclaimed and exercised his Father's healing love, and yet in a sense we have been so "mesmerized" by the life and resurrection of Jesus Christ, and by the gifts of the Holy Spirit, that we have tended to diminish the role and nature of God as our loving Father. It was he who sent his only Son as his free gift to us:

> Blessed be God the Father of our Lord Jesus Christ, who has blessed us with all the spiritual blessings of heaven in Christ. Before the world was made, he chose us, chose us in Christ, to be holy and spotless, and to live through love in his presence, determining that we should become his adopted sons, through Jesus Christ for his own kind purposes, to make us praise the glory of his grace, his free gift to us in the Beloved, in whom, through his blood, we gain our freedom, the forgiveness of our sins. (Ephesians 1:3-7).

The love that we see manifested in the compassion and caring of Jesus Christ is nothing other than the Father's love for his children. "The words I say to you I do not speak as from myself: it is the Father, living in me, who is doing this work" (John 14:10). Jesus is God the Father with a human face. He "is the image of God" (2 Corinthians 4:5), and it is in *obedience* to his Father's will, and in order to proclaim his glory, that Jesus worked all his miracles of healing. He knew God as the Father of everyone, who wanted them whole and healed, "and for anyone who is in Christ, there is a new creation; the old creation has gone, and now the new one is here. It is all God's [the Father's] work . . . God [the Father] in Christ was reconciling the world to himself, not holding men's faults against them, and he has entrusted to us the news that they are reconciled" (2 Corinthians 5:17-19). Jesus in obedience to his Father came to restore us to an awareness of his Father's unshakeable, unchangeable love for us.

In my ministry of healing I have always prayed directly and

primarily to God the Father. It is not that I exclude Christ, the healer, or ignore the power of the Holy Spirit in healing, but on the contrary, all healing ultimately makes me aware of God as a loving Father to whom Christ leads me: "No one can come to the Father except through me" (John 14:16). The Spirit alone makes me truly understand what a beautiful, generous, compassionately loving Father God really is (Romans 8:14-15). The Father is, however, the source and ultimate end of all healing, in which the Blessed Trinity is invoked and involved.

Sometimes we tend to separate our love for Christ from our love of God the Father, so that we never really experience God's love as a father. A letter from Christine puts her finger on the nub of the problem.

I am a member of a Charismatic Protestant Church. I have been to a great many wonderful services, both in my own church and others. However, I can say from the depths of my heart that never, absolutely never, have I been so powerfully and wonderfully touched by the Spirit of God as I was at the Mass for Inner Healing. I already knew the love of Jesus, but somehow the love of God the Father evaded me. I never had a loving father as a child, so when people told me to imagine the Father's love it was imposs- ible for me. I feared God and stood in awe of His might, His power, His holiness. No matter how hard I tried I could not put the whole question of sin into perspective. I longed to be like Jesus, but even with the Holy Spirit within me I fell time and time again. I wondered if God would send me to hell and I trembled. I have questioned so many people and no one could give me an answer which satisfied me. Yesterday, I saw how God sees me. The Spirit showed me before that Jesus was Lord. Now, I know in my heart that no matter what happens, God is my Father, full of mercy and compassion . . .

As Christians we love Christ because he became one of us from the cradle to the grave, but far too many of us still regard God the Father as being "another kind of Being out there", so powerful and righteous that he would not understand or condone our weakness, and in some way Christ shields us from God's anger. This spiritual attitude is destructive of God the Father's love.

If this is our way of looking at God the Father, then Christ failed in his mission on earth, which was to make the Fatherhood of God known and loved. Neither will we have received the Holy Spirit if we think like this: "Everyone moved by the Spirit is a son of God . . . and it makes us cry out 'Abba, Father'" (Romans 8:14-15). One of the greatest helps in eradicating this false notion of God, is to get those who slavishly fear a righteous God to read, slowly and meditatively, the gospel of John. If God is not a better father than the best father who ever lived, then he is not the God whom Jesus preached. "Is there a man among you who would hand his son a stone when he asked for bread? Or would hand him a snake when he asked for a fish? If you, then, who are evil, know how to give your children what is good, how much more will your Father in heaven give good things to those who ask him!" (Matthew 7:9-11).

Jesus revealed God, by word and action, as a loving Father who in his mercy heals and saves us. If there had been no merciful, loving God the Father, there would have been no Christ the Reconciler and Healer. Therefore in all my healing ministry when I am led in faith to pray for healing, of whatever type or magnitude, I have no hesitation in calling on God the Father in confidence and in total expectancy. Shades of Sister Raymond!!! "Ask, and it will be given to you", says Jesus, "search, and you will find; knock, and the door will be opened to you. For the one who asks, always receives; the one who searches always finds; the one who knocks will always have the door opened to him" (Matthew 7:7-8).

If we really believe in God as a loving Father who wants what is best for us, then our prayers for healing will take on a new dimension of trust. When suffering seems pointless we will not automatically say, "It is God's will", and convict God of being a monster, instead of praying to him and asking him "Why?" It is in this tussle with God on the battlefield of suffering that Christians grow, and the Fatherhood of God is more openly revealed and acknowledged. We must not be afraid to question God when suffering comes. It is in this questioning that a special form of healing is discovered, through which we grow.

People have gone to faith healers and spiritualists seeking healing because we as Christians have failed to minister the Gospel's healing power to the sick. For many years it has been my practice, whenever I have been called to the bed of a sick person, to pray for healing. One of the big stumbling blocks in the Christian ministry of healing is that we believe God wants us to suffer and does not ordinarily answer our prayers. I believe God *always* answers our prayers, but we have to seek in faith what his will is for every particular healing and each individual person. There will be times when we may not be led to pray for an obvious physical healing because ultimately there is a deeper inner healing of mind and soul, granted by a loving Father.

A typical example is Graham. In his early forties he was crippled with cancer of the spine. I prayed for his inner healing and that of his wife and two young children, but not for his physical healing. Over the months, I saw him fight his disease – but not alone. He knew God the Father was with him in the valley of darkness. He grew spiritually like a giant and his inner peace was tangible. Just before he died he praised God for his kindness to him, and his legacy to his family is not of tears without hope, but of deep Christian peace which continues to permeate their lives and home. Graham never doubted God the Father's love for him, and trusted me even when I told him that in faith I was not led to pray for a physical healing. In the end it was he who healed us all.

Suffering tests our faith in a loving God, and when we have explored every avenue of possible explanation we have to confess that why God allows suffering to happen is beyond our human comprehension. It is in the face of such suffering that we must hold firm to the faith that God is still our loving Father. A few months ago I went to the funeral of a young man who was struck down with a malignant tumour of the brain. Within a week of diagnosis he was dead. His parents came to one of our healing services in Tadcaster, as he lay ill in hospital. They came to pray for a healing. I suppose they wanted a physical miracle but, as so often happens, I was led to pray for inner healing of their broken spirits and shattered dreams. Twenty-four hours later, as their son, Mark, died in their arms, Pat and Billy praised God the Father for the gift of their son for twenty-five years. "I will give him back to you Father," said Pat, "and thank you for the beautiful way you have tended the wounds of our broken hearts." The priest who had just given the Sacrament of the Sick to Mark stood back in awe at such a powerful faith. Perhaps he was healed too. The only value in suffering remains the deepening of our faith and love of God the Father.

I would not even attempt to unravel the problem of pain, but I pray about it. We do not understand suffering in our own lives, our world or God's world. "Who could ever know the mind of the Lord? Who could ever be his counsellor?" (Romans 11:35). It is given to no one to understand fully the mystery of suffering in his own life. Jesus himself, as a man, shrank from personal suffering.

"Father," he said, "if you are willing, take this cup away from me. Nevertheless, your will be done, not mine" (Luke 22:42-43). Could God the Father have saved him? He did not, so why not? Was it because he wanted to show us that suffering is always a good thing, and that if his Son was prepared to suffer then so should we be? In the cruel death of his Son, did the Father wish to show us in gory detail what our sins have done to him? If you completely agree, positively, with these answers and have nothing extra to add, then your God is not my Father. There is another, deeper reason behind Christ's suffering and death.

I believe that Jesus died to show us how much he loved his Father and that he was prepared to pay the ultimate sacrifice by giving his life in testimony of that love. He died also that he could show his Father how much he loved us, even though we are sinners, because *he was one of us dying for all of us*. "He has entered the sanctuary once and for all, taking with him not the blood of goats and bull calves, but his own blood, having won an eternal redemption for us" (Hebrews 9:12). It was men not God who crucified him. Even in the affairs of his own Son, God the Father allowed men who sentenced and crucified him to abuse their free will, and for his Son to die in complete obedience and faith. When Jesus died on the cross, God the Father allowed it to happen while, as it were, "turning away his face". It is the same with every form of suffering in our lives and the lives of others.

I wonder why more hospital chaplains do not pray for physical healing of their patients. They seem to leave all "that kind of healing" to the doctors and nurses, while they persuade the patient that acceptance of the cross is Christ's basic and only message, and that suffering is what God the Father wants of us. Is it any wonder so many people turn their backs on the God who does not save because he does not care? The fatalistic "it is God's will" syndrome has done untold damage to the image of God as a loving Father. It is he who healed through Christ, and heals through us if we only learn to believe in the power of his love and mercy. Healing is essential to the spread and understanding of the Gospel. Healing is a powerful weapon of evangelization which we have almost completely discarded as obsolete, and yet God the Father's loving compassion has not lost its ancient power. In fact today, with the increase of spiritualists, faith healers, white voodoo and a thousand other so-called Christian counterfeits, it is perhaps more necessary to exercise the ministry of healing even than it was in the time of Christ.

Another common reason why God is not seen as a loving Father may be because a person has never experienced the human love of a father. A typical example is Margaret, from Waterford in Ireland. She was abandoned by her mother and left at the door of the local convent, because it was a suffocatingly destructive social stigma to be an unmarried mother. Margaret was adopted by Ellen and John, an extremely loving couple, who loved her just as much as they did their own six children. Still she fretted about her real parents, and this came between her allowing herself really to love John and Ellen and the rest of the family. She did not feel that she "belonged", and nothing could make her change her attitude. She was hurt, resenting God for allowing her to be abandoned by her natural parents. In fact, the more John and Ellen tried to make it up to her, the more she resented it and drew back into her shell.

After leaving school she met and married Sean, a gentle, caring husband, and they were blessed with three lovely children. Still she could not relax normally with her husband and children because the nagging handicap of her childhood haunted her every waking moment. One day, when visiting an orphanage, she saw a little baby boy, John, and in him she saw herself. Sean agreed to adopt him and, just as she had been loved by her adoptive parents so John was by her family. Her agony still persisted, however, and she came to me for inner healing.

Here is how she described what happened in her healing.

> Soon after you laid your hands on my head, I felt God's loving power within me. I knew I had not only to forgive my mother for abandoning me, and the father I never knew, but to love them as well, not only because they brought me into the world of my adopted parents but because they must have been under all sorts of social pressures. I thanked God for my husband and children, especially for little John. For the first time in my life I was experiencing a loving Father in my life, and my prayers and tears began to flow. I could feel a cheek against mine and little arms around my neck. When I opened my eyes I could see it was John telling me "I love you Mammy".

When his mother lay motionless in the power of the Spirit, John thought that in fact she was ill, and so he snatched himself away from those who were holding him and threw himself on his mother in floods of child's tears. It moved us all. The last time I was in Ireland on a healing mission, Margaret was one of those who assisted me, because God in turn had blessed her with the gift of healing. Her whole family and spiritual life had altered so much that I was unable to recognize her at first, she was so physically changed. She did not seem to be the same person at all, either in appearance or attitude. Then she told me the result of her healing and how her life was changed. She has a special ministry to those who are orphaned, and her teaching is of God as the Loving Father of us all. She who suffered, now helps others to know their heavenly Father as someone special who loves them.

I have found deep inner damage in people who suffer from an unhappy childhood where they are the victims of selfish, demanding, possessive parents. Because they often hate themselves, because of their inner feelings of resentment towards their parents, they are unable to relate to God as a loving Father. They have never known his earthly counterpart and so are psychologically and spiritually unable to love "the Father, from whom every family, whether spiritual or natural, takes its name" (Ephesians 3:15). Through the abuse of the word "father" in our damaged family and society, it is today true in a special sense that you "must call no one on earth your father, since you have only one Father and he is in heaven" (Matthew 23:9). Our earthly parents are only our elder brothers and sisters. A truly human Christian family is the proper setting in which God the Father can demonstrate his very special love and protection, just as he did for Jesus at his home in Nazareth, where he "increased in wisdom and stature, and in favour with God and men" (Luke 2:52).

Apart from suffering and lack of experience of a loving earthly father, another main factor militating against our belief in God as a loving father, is our wrong notion of sin and forgiveness. The false attitude to forgiveness of sin which sees God as a vengeful judge, over the centuries has done untold damage to the Gospel of Jesus on the Fatherhood of God. Fear of punishment in this life and the next means that the soul is so shrivelled, the mind so tormented and the body so suppressed, that God the Father "cannot" unloose the cage bolted by fear which is only opened from the inside. We need faith to set us free.

> Fear knocked at the door
> Faith answered
> There was no one there.

In my book *Why Are You Afraid?* I tried to analyse the fear which is one of the greatest stumbling blocks to our love of God as a Father. God wants us to be free, to be more ourselves, because it is to his glory that we are allowing ourselves to trust him with the ultimate direction of our lives. Fear breeds worry and anxiety, and this destroys our faith and trust in God's loving personal care of us. "Can any of you, for all this worrying, add one single cubit to his span of life?" (Matthew 6:27).

A typical example of what I mean was expressed in a letter from Cynthia of London.

I lived most of my life in fear, not only of the next life but of this one as well. I was afraid that all sorts of calamities would fall on me, and that I was powerless to avoid them. I had related to Jesus as a friend and felt touched by the Holy Spirit, but I was afraid, rather strangely, of God as a Father. I felt I was hiding some sins from him for which he would take me to task either in this world or most certainly in the next. Then in the healing service, I felt two hands upon my head and I knew instinctively that my heavenly Father had come to me. Since then I have received more healing and in a way, as never before, I praise God. I am free from fear to praise and thank my heavenly Father for my faith and my freedom.

Cynthia could not relate to God because of irrational feelings of guilt. She felt in some way unworthy of God's love which she had forfeited by some imaginary sins that were hidden even from herself. Like many other Christians to whom I have ministered, she felt guilty about asking for healing from her fear because she felt that the suffering she endured was sent by God as a punishment. Since Christ said we were to take up our cross daily and follow him

(Matthew 16:24), she saw her guilt and fear as part of her cross. Irrational fear and guilt have nothing to do with the Christian Gospel of forgiveness and the Fatherhood of God, and everything to do with superstition and voodooism. They are the most common diseases among people who in other respects are pillars of the institutional churches. In some cases they are so deeply ingrained in the emotional and spiritual structure of the individual that they need intensive prayer and powerful healing. The sad thing is that so many "good" people live for years in this spiritual desert, and are Christian orphans who have never known or loved their Father. The churches that teach forgiveness must also free their followers from the shackles of pagan fear and oppressive guilt, so that God as a Father may be worshipped in spirit and in truth. Fear and guilt can so permeate people's lives that no amount of preaching seems to get through to them. It is for such that Jesus came to prove that he was indeed "Master of the Sabbath" and that all the commandments can be reduced to two: "You must love the Lord your God with all your heart, with all your soul, with all your mind and with all your strength . . . You must love your neighbour as yourself. There is no commandment greater than these" (Mark 12:30-31).

Love of God and our neighbour will unblock the coldness, bitterness, the ache of bereavement, the pain of loneliness and rejection, the resentment at our ill-treatment by others, the thousand and one things that keep us so locked up in ourselves that we are unable to love even ourselves. Forgiveness of others, and of ourselves, is essentially linked with healing and the love of the Fatherhood of God. When his love flows into us then we will begin to understand more deeply the obedience of Christ, and the gifts of the Holy Spirit. Life will take on a new meaning. What occurred in the Early Church, when God was so clearly the Father of his people, can happen again in our Church and world if only we truly believe in healing. The Father of all holiness will make us whole again, and the Kingdom of Heaven will already come on earth in our life and love once we dare to call him Father, and know him by no other name.

5.

Jesus the Wounded Healer

Jesus as a person was a reconciler and healer. He did not heal as God or man, but as a person. His life was a complete and total mission of reconciliation and healing. His *whole person* brought a healing influence to a wounded world. He healed, not only through everything he said and did but even through his presence. Healing was not an extra in his life or something he did to prove his message. It *was* the message. It was an end in itself because through it he made people whole and able to live the "new life". Through his actions, words and life-style he reconciled and healed people. His healing showed that he cared about people. He healed them because he loved them, and in this he was reflecting the caring, sharing, saving love of God the Father.

"The words I say to you I do not speak as from myself: it is the Father living in me who is doing this work" (John 14:10). Jesus reconciled and healed as a sign and proof that his Father loved us and cared about us. It was as if Jesus was saying to everyone he healed, "I am healing you not only because I love you and want you to be whole, but my Father in heaven loves you so much that he is healing you through me."

His message about liberating people was actually achieved through his healing power. He did not just talk about freedom. He set people free. His healing was *ordinary* to him, in so far as this is what he came to do with his life. It was *not extraordinary* for him to make the blind see. He said that this was his mission the first time he stood up to preach in the synagogue of his youth (Luke 4:18). He proclaimed to his listeners the character of his mission, a mission which intrinsically involved healing. It was so essential to his Gospel that if you take healing out of it the message is essentially changed. Throughout his life Jesus was a healer, to such an extent that even his clothes became instruments of healing. "Now there was a woman who had suffered from a haemorrhage for twelve years; after long and painful treatment under various doctors, she had spent all she had without being any the better for it, in fact, she was getting worse. She had heard about Jesus, and she came up behind him through the crowd and touched his cloak. 'If I can touch even his clothes,' she had told herself, 'I shall be well again.' And the source of the bleeding dried up instantly" (Mark 5:25-29). Even before he could speak he was his Father's messenger of healing, evoking *joy* from John the Baptist in his mother's womb (Luke 1:44), *peace* from Simeon (Luke 2:29), and *praise* of God his Father from Anna (Luke 2:38).

Healing predominated the whole of his life and all his waking hours: "That evening, after sunset, they brought to him all who were sick and those who were possessed by devils. The whole town came crowding round the door" (Mark 1:32-33). At the end of his life, as he hung dying upon the cross, he continued his healing work, when he prayed for forgiveness for those who crucified him, promised paradise to the repentant thief, and comforted his grieving mother by bequeathing John to her to take his place. His life, whether in word or deed, was a healing life. This is what he came on earth to do in order to obey his Father's will. On the cross he said, "It is accomplished". His mission in his earthly life of healing and reconciliation was now complete (John 19:30).

Many people who read the Bible are preoccupied with using the miracles of Jesus as proofs of his divinity or as a divine guarantee that what he was saying was true and from God. I also used to interpret the Gospel in that way, but now I see Jesus' wonderful acts of healing essentially as proofs that God the Father loves us and wants us whole and healthy, able to live the new life as freed children whom he loves. I believe that Jesus did not heal solely as God, as if his human body was an appendage. He was truly a man, and healed as a man with a divine mission to heal and restore people. The Father sent Jesus on earth to heal and reconcile. He healed as he did because in his human nature he was *both* in love with God his Father and with everyone in his world. For Jesus, his healings were not "miracles" as much as "works" given to him to do by his Father in whose name and power he accomplished them. This "new" way of thinking about the healings of Jesus, in which his whole humanity is involved, has completely changed the life of a man called Brian from London.

Previously I thought only Jesus could work miracles because he was the Son of God. Now I know that he did all these wonderful things for people because he was human, one of us, and I knew that healing was what his Father wanted for us. Now my own belief in God the Father's power and willingness to heal through me in my humanity, has made me come closer to Jesus and his willingness to be so completely used by his Father. It is his loving obedience to the Father as a man, that is the real secret of healing.

Jesus, as a man, "allowed" himself to be "used" by God his Father. He loved and healed in such a liberating way that it was obvious to those around him who had open minds and hearts, that here was no ordinary man. "Here is a teaching that is new", they said, "and with authority behind it: he gives orders even to unclean spirits and they obey him"

(Mark 1:27). "They were all astounded and praised God saying, "We have never seen anything like this" (Mark 2:12). The "power" by which Jesus showed he was the Son of God was not that he worked "miracles of healing" or did "extraordinary things" in the sense that they were rare occurrences, but that healing was "ordinary" to him because he loved his heavenly Father. He also loved people, and healing was an essential pattern of this love. Of course Jesus could heal as the Son of God, but in his human nature by his *human love and his obedience* he was so perfectly attuned to his Father's will that he was able to do things no human being had ever done before.

His human love was so perfect that its source could only be divine. By loving as completely and unselfishly as he did, it was obvious that God was with him. In this powerful medium of love he showed to his onlookers that he was God's only Son, a title he so often claimed. "The Jews fetched stones to stone him, so Jesus said to them, 'I have done many good works for you to see, works from my Father; for which of these are you stoning me?' The Jews answered him, 'We are not stoning you for doing a good work but for blasphemy: you are only a man and you claim to be God' Jesus answered . . . 'If I am not doing my Father's work, there is no need to believe me; but if I am doing it, then even if you refuse to believe in me, at least believe in the work I do, then you will know for sure that the Father is in me and I am in the Father'" (John 10:31-34, 37-38). It does not detract from his dignity to stress and emphasize the human dimension of his healing work. In the sheer beauty of his selfless healing the loving goodness of his Father shone through. This was "proof" enough that he was the loving Son of a Father who loves us. "Philip said, 'Lord, let us see the Father and then we shall be satisfied'. 'Have I been with you all this time, Philip,' said Jesus to him, 'and you still do not know me?

To have seen me is to have seen the Father'" (John 14:8-9). Jesus was God's transparent love. Love was his "message and mission" from his Father, and it was this personal love that reconciled and healed, restored and renewed people. "As the Father has loved me, so I have loved you" (John 15:9). Jesus, through his healing love and his humanity, showed to people the "acceptable face" of God as a Father. "A leper came to him and pleaded on his knees: 'If you want,' he said, 'you can cure me.' Feeling sorry for him, Jesus stretched out his hand and touched him. 'Of course I want to!' he said. 'Be cured!' And the leprosy left him at once and he was cured" (Mark 1:40-41). Jesus was sorry for and healed the leper precisely because his Father was sorry for him and wanted the man healed.

It was because he was human that Jesus was able to feel sorry for the leper. His healing was his reaction to human misery, when he reached out to people and his loving *compassionate touch* healed them. He never used healing in order to say, "Look, I am healing you because I am God, and I am using you in order to show others how powerful I am!" People were never secondary to Jesus. He healed because he loved – and in fact often forbade people to tell others about their healing: "He warned them strongly not to tell others about it" (Mark 3:12). The time was not right for them to do so. He healed because they needed healing. In their brief encounter with Jesus, those whom he healed knew that in some mysterious way, which they could not understand, *God was touching and healing them*. It was important at that particular time for them to be healed, and "the time would come" when they could proclaim that the source and power of their healing was Jesus of Nazareth.

He healed people for their own sake and this has always seemed more important and loving to me, than healing them in order to prove the authenticity of his divine mission. I am highly suspicious of "healers" who *look* for signs and wonders among their "audience" as a divine confirmation of their *own* special powers and ministry, rather than as tangible evidence that God the Father loved people, was healing them through Christ and was using the minister as an instrument of the Holy Spirit's power on their behalf. "Then some of the scribes and Pharisees spoke up. 'Master,' they said, 'we should like to see a sign from you.' Jesus replied, 'It is an evil and unfaithful generation that asks for a sign!'" (Matthew 12:38-39), although signs and wonders will follow those who believe: "These are the signs that will be associated with believers: in my name they will cast out devils; they will have the gift of tongues; they will pick up snakes in their hands, and be unharmed should they drink deadly poison; they will lay their hands on the sick, who will recover" (Mark 16:17-18).

Whenever I minister in healing, I see myself as the servant of the Father dispensing his healing love as he wills to whom he wills. It is not anything of mine over which I have absolute possession or control. All healing is a sign of the love of God the Father, who wants to heal and reconcile us through his Son: "It was God who reconciled us to himself through Christ and gave us the work of handing on this reconciliation" (2 Corinthians 5:18). Jesus heals through us so that in the healing ministry we may show forth the Father's willingness and power to make people whole, in order that they can live the new life of grace and fulfilment. The healing ministry is a proclamation of the Father's love.

The reason I stress the humanity of Jesus in his healing ministry is because so many Christians restrict his healing powers to his divinity. Of course, Jesus could heal everyone of all their diseases, spiritual, emotional, physical, or even cast out devils, because he was God. Yet if we truly believe in the Incarnation, and that "he did not cling to his equality with God but emptied himself to assume the condition of a slave" (Philippians 2:6-7), then surely his humanity played a special role in every aspect of his life.

In every case of healing, *Jesus as a person healed the person who came to him in faith.* His healing was of the whole person when his world made contact with the world of the person who needed to be healed: "The word was made flesh, he lived among us and we saw his glory" (John 1:14), the glory that was made visible by his loving ministry of healing people because he was one of them. He was the brother come to bring new life and hope to the human family. When we look again at the works of Jesus we will see how often he calls on the Father in prayer to confirm his loving mission by healing. "Father, I thank you for hearing my prayer. I knew indeed that you always hear me, but I speak for the sake of all these who stand round me, so that they may believe it was you who sent me" (John 11:41-42). Is that anything other than a "human" prayer? It is no different to the prayer used constantly today by people who exercise Christ's healing ministry.

Because Jesus, as a person, healed persons, he healed whatever needed healing in them. *There was no priority in the scale of his healing.* Many people so restrict his healing to that of personal sin that they see his physical healing as secondary and less important. This attitude is totally alien to the Gospel and to the healing ministry of Jesus. Take the classical example of the paralytic (Matthew 9:1-8). Was Jesus showing a priority of sin over the physical disability of the person before him? If this were the case then as a person he did not really humanly care about physical suffering so extreme that the person had to be carried everywhere by his friends. No! In the case of the paralytic whose sins he healed first, he was showing his discernment of the paralytic's real and most pressing need. He then physically healed him in order to show he had power over both forms of illnesses. Would he have healed him of sin and left him paralysed? This way of thinking is in contradiction to Jesus' way of acting. The whole person was the object of his love, and physical illness was as great an evil as sin itself. He healed both the sin and the paralysis because he loved the person lying before him on a stretcher.

In short, Jesus showed his love for God and man by healing every form of sickness, whether it was spiritual, emotional or physical. He saw sickness as a result of sin which he came to conquer, and whenever he was approached *in faith* by anyone, for healing for themselves or others, *he never refused*. Even though he forgave sin on numerous occasions, nevertheless the gospels contain more accounts of physical healing than of any other type. Jesus helped the suffering in whatever way they needed. Often it was not in the way they or their neighbours might have expected, as in the case of the paralytic (Matthew 9:1-8), but his healing was always for the health of the whole person in this life and the next.

I stress the human aspect of Jesus' healing because this is absolutely essential to all those who are privileged to serve God in the ministry of healing. Jesus healed as a man, or in his humanity, because he allowed God the Father to work through him. If we are to appreciate our own ministry of healing and understand how God works through us then we need to meditate on the outstanding healing aspects of Jesus' life, and try to live them out in our own lives. To study the life of Jesus is to study the mystery and ministry of healing. Every minister of healing is "another Christ". If there is any part of his life which is not rooted in Christ then his ministry will disintegrate and dry up.

From my own experience of the ministry, all healing is based on *God's love for us which overflows from us to other people* so that in the process they are healed. This was the secret power of Jesus' healing love. "I say this to you, said Jesus: love your enemies and pray for those who persecute you; in this way you will be sons of your Father in heaven" (Matthew 5:44-45). "My dear people, let us love one another since love comes from God and everyone who loves is begotten by God and knows God. Anyone who fails to love can never have known God, because God is love. God's love for us was revealed when God sent into the world his only Son so that we could have life through him; this is the love I mean: not our love for God, but God's love for us when he sent his Son to be the sacrifice that takes our sins away. My dear people, since God has loved us so much, we too should love one another" (1 John 4:7-11). Unless we really love the person to be healed then there will be no healing on our part. By love I do not mean a sloppy, sentimental, emotional love, but a deep awareness that the person in need of healing is a child of God the Father who wants to heal them, and is willing to use us as his instruments. There must be no barriers of hate or distrust between us.

The secret of Jesus' healing was *love in action* which placed no limits within itself. The limits came from outside. No one was excluded from his healing love, except those who excluded themselves through closed minds and hearts and lack of faith. "Jesus went to his home town [of Nazareth] . . . With the coming of the sabbath he began teaching in the synagogue and most of them were astonished when they heard him. They said, 'Where did this man get all this? What is this wisdom that has been granted him, and these miracles that are worked through him? This is the carpenter, surely, the son of Mary . . .' And they would not accept him. And Jesus said to them, 'A prophet is only despised in his own country, among his own relations and in his own house'; and he could work no miracle there, though he cured a few sick people by laying his hands on them. He was amazed at their lack of faith" (Mark 6:1-6).

Jesus loved his Father so much that they were as one in mind and purpose. His human love was such that he entered into his Father's mind and heart. He knew his Father wanted people healed, made whole, so that they could live the New Life, and his love for the Father which flowed out to them was healing and liberating. It was the Father's love which healed, because Jesus in his humanity placed no barrier between himself and his Father. This *openness in love* is the secret power and source of all Christian healing. It was this openness in love to the Father, and therefore to each other, that Jesus prayed would be the outstanding mark of his followers: "Father may they [the disciples] be one in us, as you are in me and I am in you" (John 17:21). "By this love you have for one another, everyone will know that you are my disciples" (John 13:35).

Besides his unique love for his Father and people, Jesus also had the most special kind of *faith and trust* in God his Father. As a rule we have not appreciated how deep was Jesus' faith, how complete his trust and how necessary they were for his ministry of healing. There are those who so dehumanize Jesus that he is left bereft of faith, because in their theology he knows everything and does not need faith. It would certainly be strange that a person who put such emphasis on the necessity of faith, so that he could accomplish his mission of healing, should himself have no need to believe. It was as if Jesus were saying in his acts of healing, "You lesser mortals have to believe that I have the power to heal you, because if not, I will withdraw it and leave you in your miserable state. As for me, I can do anything because I am the Son of God and don't need any kind of faith, for I know that when I say to someone 'Be healed!' he is healed just because I say so without reference to anyone else!" By his own life Jesus gave us an example of how we should live, and if we were to take faith out of Jesus' life then we would be left with an empty shell of a man and a parody of the Gospel.

Jesus had *conviction* when he healed. He had authority over devils, he even rebuked physical diseases, because through his intensely penetrating, discerning faith he "knew" that this was what his Father wanted him to do. In this way he showed his total obedience in love to his Father, who was glorified by what happened. By his own conviction he emphasized the necessity of faith and gave an example to future Christians of the power of faith in the healing ministry.

This was brought forcibly home to me by Brian, who today exercises a very powerful healing ministry in London. "If Jesus knew everything", he said, "and did not need faith, then it was 'easy' for him to heal. He *knew* what would happen. It must have been 'easy' for him to suffer and die because he *knew* he would rise again and he knew what heaven was like."

Jesus stepped out in faith time and again to heal in his public life, and never once did God the Father let him down. In a special sense Jesus had more faith than any person ever born, and he encouraged faith in all his disciples. "Then Jesus got into the boat followed by his disciples. Without warning a storm broke over the lake, so violent that the waves were breaking right over the boat. But he was asleep. So they went to him and woke him saying, 'Save us, Lord, we are going down!' And he said to them, 'Why are you so frightened, you men of little faith?' And with that he stood up and rebuked the winds and the sea; and all was calm again. The men were astounded and said 'Whatever kind of man is this? Even the winds and the sea obey him'" (Matthew 8:23-27).

By his divinity, Jesus could, in his own right, have calmed the winds and the sea, but if, as St Paul says, "he did not cling to his equality with God" (Philippians 2:6) then it was as a man of faith that he saved the disciples from drowning. His faith was set against their fear, and through his faith he taught them a lesson, that the faith which could move mountains would also calm the winds and the sea. "Then the disciples came privately to Jesus. 'Why were we unable to cast the devil out?' they asked. He answered, 'Because you have little faith. I tell you solemnly, if your faith were the size of a mustard seed you could say to this mountain, 'Move from here to there', and it would move; nothing would be impossible for you" (Matthew 17:19-20). This means that if we really believed, then there would be no limit to our healing mission.

As well as his total obedience, Jesus so loved his Father that he lived out his life in complete *trust*, doing whatever the Father wanted him to do. Healing was the work of the Kingdom, the business of his Father. He put healing before his own tiredness or any form of personal suffering. From the age of twelve, when he emerged from the Temple with the illuminating conviction that "he must be about his Father's business" (Luke 2:50), until his death on the cross, when he commended his spirit to his Father, Jesus gave an example of how we should live. We live for the Kingdom. His advice to his followers was not just mere words, but was lived out in practice in every aspect of his own life. "Set your hearts on God's kingdom first, and on his right-eousness, and all these other things will be given you as well. So do not worry about tomorrow: tomorrow will take care of itself. Each day has enough trouble of its own" (Matthew 6:33-34). Trust is the opposite side of the coin of faith. Whenever Jesus was called to heal, once he dis-cerned through prayer what his Father wanted him to do, he did it, and then left the result to his Father. Unlike Moses he never struck the rock twice. This trust left Jesus in command in every healing situation.

A typical example of this authority and confidence is to be found in the raising of Lazarus from the dead (John 11:41-44). It begins with a prayer of thanksgiving to his Father, followed by a prayer of intercession. Then comes the *voice of authority*. "Lazarus, here! Come out! . . . Unbind him, let him go free." Jesus was always in constant, sensitive communication with his Father through prayer, which was central to his healing mission. *All healing flows from prayer* and gives it the ring of authenticity. Jesus believed that when, in faith and trust, he prayed to his Father his requests were granted. "Ask, and it will be given to you; search, and you will find; knock, and the door will be opened to you. For the one who asks always receives; the one who searches always finds; the one who knocks will always have the door opened to him" (Matthew 7:7-8). The promise is there for all his followers, limited only by their faith. The tragedy is that our prayer, like our faith, is too shallow and selfish. Jesus put no limits to his Father's healing love, even to raising people from the dead, and he himself has promised, "I tell you most solemnly, whoever believes in me will perform the same works as I do myself, he will perform even greater works, because I am going to the Father. Whatever you ask for in my name I will do, so that the Father may be glorified in the Son. If you ask for anything in my name, I will do it" (John 14:12-14). Prayer opens us up to God and to the discovery of our real selves. In the very asking we find a healing.

Jesus is ultimately our healer because "being as all men are, he was humbler yet, even to accepting death, death on a cross" (Philippians 2:7-8). Jesus is our *wounded healer*. "He was bearing our own faults in his own body on the cross, so that we might die to our faults and live for holiness: *through his wounds you have been healed*" (1 Peter 2:24). Jesus reconciles and heals us because through his suffering and death he enters into our problems and sufferings, and through his resurrection we share in his victory over sin and death. The great reconciling and healing sacrament of his Church is baptism, for "when we were baptized in Christ Jesus we were baptized in his death; . . . so that as Christ was raised from the dead by the Father's glory, we too might live a new life" (Romans 6:3-4).

Just as Jesus' sufferings have meaning only in the light of the resurrection, so all human suffering truly finds its fulfilment in wholeness, healing and living the new life. Suffering for Jesus is not something positive or an end in itself. If it were then why did he heal so many thousands of people? He acknowledged the inevitability of suffering just as truly as he was aware of the pervading presence of sin. He did not seek suffering, nor as a man did he fully understand its mystery in his Father's plan of salvation. Even on the night before he died he prayed: "My Father," he said, "if it is possible, let this cup pass me by. Nevertheless, let it be as you, not I, would have it" (Matthew 26:39). The fact, that Jesus was prepared to suffer so much as a man, because of his love for his Father and for us, without knowing in detail all its circumstances, has been for countless Christians a source of great healing and inner strength. The most moving account of Jesus' total surrender in death is surely that of Isaiah.

> God has been pleased to crush him with suffering.
> If he offers his life in atonement,
> he shall see his heirs, he shall have a long life
> and through him what God wishes will be done.
>
> His soul's anguish over
> he shall see the light and be content.
> By his sufferings shall my servant justify many,
> taking their faults on himself.

Hence I will grant whole hordes for his tribute,
he shall divide the spoil with the mighty,
for surrendering himself to death
and letting himself be taken for a sinner,
while he was bearing the faults of many
and praying all the time for sinners (Isaiah 53:10-12).

Jesus did not attempt to explain suffering, but admitted that each day has enough trouble of its own (Matthew 6:34). He saw the proper use of suffering as being set into the life pattern of all his followers. "If anyone wants to be a follower of mine, let him renounce himself and take up his cross every day and follow me" (Luke 9:23). What that *proper use* of suffering is, I shall attempt to explain in a later chapter.

Every person engaged in the ministry of healing is not aloof from those around him. He too is wounded and feels for others *in compassion*. In every healing session in which I have engaged I am often overwhelmed by the sense of pain around me. In suffering we discover a sympathy with the person to be healed. Just as in prayers Jesus shared his Father with us – "You should pray like this: '*Our* Father in heaven'" (Matthew 6:9) – so he also shares our sufferings because he became a man like us in everything except sin. "For our sake God made the sinless one into sin so that in him we might become the goodness of God" (2 Corinthians 5:21). "During his life on earth, Jesus offered up prayer and entreaty, aloud and in silent tears, to the one who had the power to save him out of death, and he submitted so humbly that his prayer was heard. Although he was Son, he learnt to obey through suffering; but having been made perfect, he became for all who obey him the source of eternal salvation" (Hebrews 5:7-9). "Christ has entered the sanctuary once and for all, taking with him not the blood of goats and bull calves, but his own blood, having won an eternal redemption for us . . . He brings a new covenant, as the mediator, only so that the people who were called to an eternal inheritance may actually receive what was promised: his death took place to cancel the sins that infringed the earlier covenant" (Hebrews 9:12,15).

Jesus the wounded healer *reconciles* us to:-

God our Father
There is only one mediator between God and mankind, himself a man, Christ Jesus (1 Timothy 2:5).

Each other
In Christ Jesus, you that used to be so far apart from us have been brought very close, by the blood of Christ. For he is the peace between us (Ephesians 2:13-14).

Our own selves
For anyone who is in Christ, there is a new creation; the old creation has gone, and now the new one is here (2 Corinthians 5:17).

He *heals* us in
Soul
Your sins are forgiven (Luke 7:48).
Spirit
My own peace I give you (John 14:27).
Body
I am the resurrection. If anyone believes in me, even though he dies he will live (John 11:25).

By his whole person and way of life, by every facet of his relationship with God and with those whom he met, Jesus accomplished his task of being the world's reconciler and healer. His loving obedience to his Father, his faith and trust in him, his compassion, every form of his suffering, even rejection by his own people, prepared him and our world for the final act of reconciliation and healing.

> But God raised him high
> and gave him the name
> which is above all other names
> so that all beings
> in the heaven, on earth and in the underworld,
> should bend the knee at the name of Jesus
> and that every tongue should acclaim
> Jesus Christ as Lord,
> to the Glory of God the Father (Philippians 2:9-11).

6.

The Spirit Who Heals

God the Father loves us, and has done so from the very moment that he created the human race. Because he loves us in such a unique way as a Father, He made us in his own image and likeness: "God fashioned man of dust from the soil. Then he breathed into his nostrils a breath of life, and thus man became a living being" (Genesis 2:7). The very breath of life we breathe is his gift to us: "God's breath it was that made me, the breathing of Shaddai that gave me life" (Job 33:4). The Father gave us the "kiss of life" so that deep within us we would live *his* life. We were destined to live forever in his love and sharing. We were the most special of all his creation, the people he had chosen to love. We were his children and his friends. He gave us the earth for our inheritance: "Be fruitful, multiply, fill the earth and conquer it" (Genesis 1:28).

But as we know, it all went so sadly wrong when we abused our freedom. Yet because he is our Father, God has never ceased from loving us. If he did, then he would not be our Father. It is we who have got things wrong, and we could not readjust the focus of our life and destiny without his free and generous help. God the Father, in his love, wants to heal us. This never-failing love of God as a Father is something that is indispensable to the whole process of Christian healing. When we lose sight of God as a loving Father then healing is practically impossible. The perpetual *loving Fatherhood of God is a* condicio sine qua non *of all healing*. I have encountered hundreds of cases where I have been unable to minister in healing because those for whom

I prayed did not really believe that God loved them or wanted to heal them. This unChristian attitude tends to lead to despair and fatalism.

God the Father sent his only Son on a mission of healing love, and his love as a Father shone through Jesus' life: "The people that walked in darkness have seen a great light" (Isaiah 9:11). Everything Jesus said and did gave a new dimension to our lives because it was said or done out of love for his Father and for us. He loved his Father with a perfect human love, and he allowed his Father's divine love to come through him to us as through an unblocked channel. This love was for our healing. Jesus was Lord not only of all creation, as the Father intended he should be, but he was also Lord of our lives. His love united and reconciled us to his Father, to each other, and within ourselves. His physical life was short among us but he gave us a new pattern for human life. It could be summed up in one word – love.

God the Father and Jesus his Son wanted that pattern of life and healing love to continue, and so Jesus promised, "I shall ask the Father, and he will give you another Advocate to be with you for ever . . . The Advocate, the Holy Spirit, whom the Father will send in my name, will teach you everything and remind you of all I have said to you" (John 14:16,26). He gave us this Spirit to be our new life. Just as the Father breathed life into man at the beginning of his creation, so now the risen Jesus would breathe the new life of grace into his followers, who would preach and live by his Gospel of reconciliation and healing: "As the Father sent me, so am I sending you." After saying this he *breathed* on them and said, "Receive the Holy Spirit". "For those whose sins you forgive they are forgiven, for those whose sins you retain they are retained" (John 20:21-23). We are a new creation, restored, healed, forgiven, destined to lead the good life of wholeness and holiness, as the Father from the beginning intended that we should (Ephesians 1:3-7).

Because of the Father's love which wants to heal us, and the victory of Jesus Christ the wounded healer, they both send the Holy Spirit on all believers to live the new life and to continue the work of healing in love, begun so wonderfully in Jesus' physical life on earth. In this way the Blessed Trinity is at work in every act of healing and in every aspect of our Christian life. "Didn't you realize that you were God's temple and that the Spirit of God was living among you?" (Corinthians 3:16). We are missioners with the same mission as God the Son, of reconciliation and healing, and this mission was the outstanding characteristic of his followers in the Early Church. "The apostles continued to testify to the resurrection of the Lord Jesus with great power. The many miracles and signs worked through the apostles made a deep impression on everyone" (Acts 4:33, 2:43). They could do all these things because they were empowered by the Holy Spirit with the life of the Risen and Ascended Lord, in whose likeness they grew more and more. This Lord is the Spirit and where the Spirit of the Lord is, there is freedom. "And we, with our unveiled faces reflecting like mirrors the brightness of the Lord, all grow brighter and brighter as we are turned into the image that we reflect: this is the work of the Lord who is Spirit" (2 Corinthians 3:18).

We are living today in the last stage of the history of the world's salvation. It is the wonderful age of the Spirit who restores us to the new life of God's children and, like the Prodigal Son *who never really knew his father before*, we have returned from death to life. "If Christ is in you then your spirit is life itself because you have been justified" (Romans 8:11). The Spirit lives in us through Christ's victory over sin and death in obedience to the Father's will, and is for our healing and reconciliation. *The Spirit is in a very special sense the healer and giver of healing until the end of time.*

Through his power we are able to look on God as our loving Father, and the Risen Christ as Lord of our lives. "Everyone moved by the Spirit is a son of God. The spirit you received is not the spirit of slaves bringing fear into your lives again; it is the spirit of sons, and it makes us cry out, 'Abba, Father!' The Spirit himself and our spirit bear united witness that we are children of God. And if we are children we are heirs as well: heirs of God and coheirs with Christ, sharing his sufferings so as to share his glory" (Romans 8:14-17). By reading the Bible we can know God as a Father, but what kind of a Father? – a just judge, a rewarder of good deeds, an aloof Creator? Yet unless we really love him with true, warm love which penetrates our whole being, we will not know him at all as the Father he really is.

Let me give you an example. Mary, from our healing group, was brought up in a very strict Methodist background. She never missed her Sunday services, which she thoroughly enjoyed. She was a Sunday school teacher and a prominent, active member of her local church. She was everything a Methodist could desire. She was the leader of a flourishing prayer group, and for two years she helped me in the healing ministry. Yet I felt there was something missing in her Christian life, as if she were being held back by invisible bonds which prevented her from experiencing the full freedom and joy of being a Christian. One Sunday morning, as we were preparing in prayer for the afternoon's healing session, I spoke about God as our loving Father and how much we needed him. Suddenly Mary literally cried out the words "Abba, Father" in anguish or so I thought, but it was the sheer joy of realizing for the first time that God was really a Father who loved her for herself and wanted everything that was best for her in her life. She was touched by his love, and her ministry has grown immeasurably since. She is a changed person in the sense that there is a freedom and joy in her spirit, a new dimension to her whole life and a greater sense of discernment and compassion in her healing ministry. The Spirit changed Mary and we all know it. There have been many other people like Mary whom I have seen released and healed by the Spirit, released from being good, ordinary church-going people to fulfilled, deeply peaceful Christians with a strong sense of mission and commitment. There can be no evangelization without the inner healing of the Spirit. We may think we know God's love as a Father, but until the Spirit comes then our assent to this liberating truth is in our minds and not in our hearts. "The proof that you are sons is that God has sent the Spirit of his Son into our hearts: the Spirit that cries out, 'Abba, Father', and it is this that makes you a son" (Galatians 4:6).

The beginning of all healing is that God is our loving Father. Once we believe in our hearts that he loves us and wants us whole, then we remove from our lives the obstacle of *fear* which destroys our freedom and trust in a loving God, who desires to share his life and happiness with us. The Spirit of Christ, the glorified Son, fills our being with this love and, in a way which we cannot explain, we know and experience God as a loving Father. It is impossible to combine the love of a son with the fear of a slave: "God is love and anyone who lives in love lives in God, and God lives in him . . . In love there can be no fear, but fear is driven out by perfect love: because to fear is to expect punishment, and anyone who is afraid is still imperfect in love. We are to love, then, because he loved us first" (1 John 4:16, 18-19). This love is Christ's gift to us in his Spirit, and through the power of his resurrection he overcomes all our fears so that we are filled with his triumph and his gratitude to his Father. By his loving obedience to his Father, *Jesus won back for us our freedom to love and to serve God in freedom*. "When Christ freed us, he meant us to remain free. Stand firm, therefore, and do not submit again to the yoke of slavery" (Galatians 5:1).

Love and freedom are correlatives in all Christian healing. God the Father always respects our freedom, and the Spirit of God brings Christ's love back into our lives again, so that, wounded in Christ, we come to our loving Father's home where there is healing and wholeness. We love and obey the Father with his Son's love. Our human person is basically healed by love, so that all the other healings, whether they be spiritual, emotional or physical, will follow as a consequence. I could recount innumerable stories of the wonderful healings that have happened once God has become "Abba, Father" of people's lives. One quite startling instance was of John, suffering from the last stages of terminal cancer. As soon as I laid hands on him for healing and prayed for him to experience God as a loving Father, he felt a burning sensation in his body where the cancer was, and a freedom of spirit which he had never known before. Today he is completely healed both in body and spirit, and I have no doubt that it was because he acknowledged God as his loving Father. And since it is only by the power of the Spirit that we have access to the Father (Ephesians 2:18), then ultimately it is the Spirit whose power enables us to be healed. This is why we look on the love of the Spirit as the power-house of healing.

As well as loving God as our Father, we need in all our healing to proclaim *Jesus as Lord* of our lives. He is the healer, wounded for our sins, whom God raised high, "and gave him the name which is above all other names . . . and that every tongue should acclaim Jesus Christ as Lord to the Glory of God the Father" (Philippians 2:9,11). This acknowledgement, not only that Christ is Lord but that he has ultimately won the victory over all our faults and illnesses, is again the work of the Holy Spirit. "No man can say Jesus is Lord unless he is under the influence of the Holy Spirit" (1 Corinthians 12:3). By "Lordship" I mean that, like Jesus in his lifetime, we model ourselves on him and live out our lives in union with his loving surrender to his Father, who in his turn crowned him as the "Lord of life". The Spirit teaches us, in a way that no one else can, what Jesus would do in each particular situation in which we find ourselves.

I never cease to be amazed at the number of times when what seemed to many people to be insuperable problems were solved or reduced to their proper size once they allowed Jesus to be Lord of the situation. This confidence, in itself a great healing, is the work of the Holy Spirit by which we really commit our lives to the Lord Jesus and his Father. "Do not let your hearts be troubled", said Jesus. "Trust in God still and trust in me" (John 14:1). The healing Spirit is always moving us through the Risen Christ to the Father. The twin aspects of the Fatherhood of God and the Lordship of Christ are both essential for healing, and are exclusively the work and gift of the Holy Spirit, so that we can truly say that it is the Spirit who heals.

In every aspect of the Christian life, but especially that of healing, there is an absolute necessity for *prayer*, and it is the Holy Spirit who is the source and inspiration of all our prayer. The presence of the Spirit within us enables us to pray to the Father as sons. Like Jesus, we trust him with our lives because on this earth we will never know fully the mystery of God's dealings with us personally in his plan for our salvation. When we are faced with the most terrible tragedies in people's lives, or in our own, and we are desperately searching for words which will heal or soothe, then it is best to be silent and allow the Holy Spirit to lead and guide us. In all my prayers of healing I find that the only prayers which flow and have a great healing effect are those which are Spirit-inspired, without any "planning" on my part. It is easy to discern when people are praying in specially couched terms which they have used countless times before, and which they are repeating just one more time over someone, without any special regard to the uniqueness of the individual concerned.

When we pray over someone the Spirit will gently open us to the person who asks for healing, and there will be a union of spirits between us. Sometimes we will have no verbal prayer to offer, at other times it may be just a few words, but always, if it is of the Holy Spirit, the prayer will heal. "The Spirit too comes to help us in our weakness. For when we cannot choose words in order to pray properly, the Spirit himself expresses our plea in a way that could never be put into words, and God, who knows everything in our hearts, knows perfectly well what he means, and that the pleas of the saints expressed by the Spirit are according to the mind of God" (Romans 8:26-27). The secret of prayers of healing is that they are few, gentle, sincere, trustful and open to the Spirit. I have been quite dismayed, at times when people pray over me, that everyone in the group feels they ought to "have a go". If one prayer is effective that is all that needs to be said. It is Spirit-filled and Christ himself, at the right hand of God, will make effective intercession for us. If we really loved God as a Father we would not feel the need to badger him with lengthy prayer in marathon sessions. God knows what is in our hearts and the Spirit will speak for us. Each situation is different. The Spirit will fill our healing prayers with the gifts of wisdom and knowledge. They will be prayers of healing peace which calm our hearts and minds.

The ministry of healing is enriched by the *gift of faith*: "to another again the gift of faith given by the same Spirit"

(1 Corinthians 12:9). All Christians have the *virtue* of faith in the sense that we believe in God, his love for us and his willingness to save us, but the gift of faith bestowed freely on us by the Holy Spirit is something very special given to those who minister in healing. It is very closely linked with the other gifts of the Holy Spirit, of *discernment* and the *word of knowledge.* It inspires us to know when to pray for someone, what to pray for, whether or not they will be healed or need more prayers of healing. This gift was eminently found in Jesus during his life on earth, and when we study the gospels we will see how beautifully he used words and prayers to heal. Two perfect examples are to be found in his dialogue with the Samaritan woman by Jacob's well (John 4:7-26), and with Nicodemus (John 3:1-21). The gift of faith, as we have said, is given by the Holy Spirit and in a later chapter we will discuss in more detail the relationship of faith to healing.

Allied to the gift of faith is the *gift of healing* (1 Corinthians 12:9). While it is true that all Christians are healers by the very fact that they are Christians, yet not all are called to the ministry of healing or given the special gifts of the Holy Spirit required for such a ministry. Nevertheless we very much under-use our capacity for healing each other within and outside the Christian community. I know of hundreds of cases where families heal each other, and so at healing sessions I anoint the hands of husbands and wives, their children, brothers and sisters, close friends and relatives, so that in laying hands on their loved ones, they may receive the power of the Spirit for this individual person and occasion. In Waterford a nun asked me to pray for her brother in the United States, from whom she had not had any news for a long time. I anointed her hands and prayed that the Spirit would give her any gifts she might require for her brother's healing. Some months later she received a letter informing her that her brother had been involved in a serious car accident which cost him his sight in both eyes. Remembering her anointing she got permission from her superiors to fly out to the Mid-West, and there in the hospital ward she laid her hands on her brother's eyes, praying for his eyesight to be restored. Her prayer was heard, and the sight in both eyes was restored. His faith, which was weak, was strengthened too and his whole life was changed. I do not think that this nun has a special ministry of healing just because of this one occasion, but I have known the ministry of healing develop from such special circumstances.

In short, all the work and gifts of the Spirit are directed towards helping us, and the community, to live out the Gospel of Jesus on the loving Fatherhood of God in our modern world. I could enumerate the various gifts of the Spirit (as outlined in 1 Corinthians 12), and how they should be used (1 Corinthians 14), but my main purpose in this chapter is to place the healing action of the Holy Spirit in the context of the Blessed Trinity. I shall deal later with the special gifts of the Holy Spirit and how they affect healing. God the Father wants to heal us, and for this reason he sent his son Jesus on earth for a short time to heal and reconcile us, and today they both send the Holy Spirit on us so that we can continue the Blessed Trinity's work of healing our wounded and broken world.

The Spirit *reconciles* us to —

1. **God our Father**
by giving us the gift of calling him "Abba" lovingly.
2. **Each other**
by giving us the grace to "forgive each other as soon as a quarrel begins. The Lord has forgiven you; now you must do the same. Over all these clothes, to keep them together and complete them, put on love" (Colossians 3:13-14)
3. **Our true Christian selves**
so that we are a new creation in the sense that through the Spirit we acknowledge Jesus Christ as Lord of our lives.

The Spirit *heals* us in —

1. Our souls
because every movement of repentance is inspired by him.

2. Our emotions
because his love fills our being and drives out fear, guilt, hurtful memories and all those elements within us which prevent us from living to the full the new life of grace.

3. Our bodies
because Jesus, who healed so many people of physical illnesses in his life, promised us that "the believer will perform the same works as I do myself, he will perform even greater works" (John 14:12).

We live in the age of the Spirit, and in his power we are called to reconcile and heal. This we do in his love which sets us free to do God's work and flows in and through our being. Our healing is effective because we do it in the Spirit of the Risen Christ. If we live the life of the Spirit then God the Father and Son will live in us. Nothing will be impossible to us because it is not impossible to them.

> Whatever we ask God
> we shall receive,
> because we keep his commandments
> and live the kind of life he wants.
> His commandments are these:
> that we believe in the name of his Son Jesus Christ
> and that we love one another
> as he told us to.
> Whoever keeps his commandments
> lives in God and God lives in him.
> We know that he lives in us
> by the Spirit that he has given us (1 John 3:23-24).

7.

Our Healing with God

God the Father loves each one of us individually as a person. Just as we are physically unique in our world and known by our fingerprints, so God knows each one of us as persons, each with a different infra-structure and background: "See I have branded you on the palms of my hands" (Isaiah 49:16). Each human person is physically and emotionally unique because the human body is a very complicated, integrated mechanism, and the emotions are much more finely tuned and intricate than the most highly-developed computer system. The only one who knows all about how we "tick" and why, is God. He knows us better than we know ourselves. He alone knows what is wrong with us as persons, and heals us in the various ways we need so that we can become whole persons again. God heals the person, and if the healing that is needed for the wholeness of the person is physical, then he heals the person physically.

Most writers on healing divide and compartmentalize the human person into specific categories of soul, emotions and body. This is a "tidy" and clinical way of analysing and synthesizing healing, but the human person in his own right is more than the sum total of all his "components", which interact because they are inter-dependent within the unity of the person. It is the wholeness of the person which is the aim of all Christian healing. No healing is so completely physical that it does not affect our emotions and our soul, it affects us as a whole person.

Let me give you a simple example of what I mean.

During a healing session in Ireland, I ministered to a young nun in her early thirties. Sister Alphonsus was so crippled with arthritis, especially her hands, that she was unable to work with the handicapped children in her charge.

From my teenage years I wanted to work with severely handicapped children who needed to be fed, clothed and have practically everything done for them. In this way, I believed that I was giving glory to God the Father, but now I am as severely handicapped myself as the children. I have been to several doctors, and they told me nothing could be done for me. Many priests and nuns tried to comfort me by assuring me that in my crippled state I was giving more glory to God in a hidden way, than any work I could do for the handicapped children. I have never accepted that because I believed it was not God's will for me, and so I have always prayed for physical healing.

After we had prayed together, during which time she surrendered her whole life, including her grave disability, to God, I touched her hands, which opened as gently as a flower budding forth in blossom. They were immediately healed. Today she is a joy to her community. Before her healing, relations between them had become very strained. Now her prayer life is full of praise and thanks to God her loving Father, and her dedication to the children is a source of joy and edification to everyone. The physical healing affected her whole person and every aspect of her life.

Conscious of this interaction within the human person, I have decided to treat healing, not so much under its usual headings of spiritual, emotional and physical, but rather under the aspect of relationships. The three main areas are:

1. Our healing with God
2. Our healing with each other
3. Our healing within ourselves

I am well aware of the interwoven pattern within the human framework, so that no area is exclusive of the others. The advantage of this treatment of healing under the aspect of relationships lies in maintaining the unity and integrity of the human person's uniqueness and identity, rather than dividing him up into body, emotions and soul, which tend to be separate entities in people's minds. It is the entire person who is healed, whether his healing be spiritual, emotional or physical.

The most important healing in our relationship with God the Father is the continuing realization that his love for us is uniquely special and never-ending. His relationship with us is personal, intimate and unique. Our response to him should have the same characteristics, but in the vast majority of cases, even among regular church-going people, this is not so. I can say this without fear of contradiction, as a result not only of my own upbringing and spiritual experience, but from thirty-five years' ministry in parishes and renewal centres covering a wide spectrum not only of Roman Catholics, but of other Christian denominations. *God is not personally loved as the Father should be loved*, as disclosed to us in the life of Christ, and the writings of St Paul. True, he is acknowledged by baptized Christians as the one true God who will reward the good and punish the wicked, but is he acknowledged to be so personal a God as to be our constant companion, helper and the one to whom we trust everything in our life, as Jesus said we should (Matthew 6:25-34)? I often ask so-called Christian people "Who is your God?", and the answers I get back are very far removed from the personal Father whom Jesus loved and of whom he preached. There can be no real spiritual progress in the Christian life until Jesus' Father is known and loved as Jesus knew and loved him. He loved him as a *personal Father*, and we must do the same. *The greatest healing needed today in all the Christian churches is the healing with God the Father.*

But what about the sacrament of baptism? Surely this makes us aware of God's personal love as our Father? What need have we of anything else? This is a whole area of theology which needs exploring if we are to relate the Spirit given in baptism with the Spirit which makes us call God "Abba, Father". Does baptism give us the Holy Spirit in such a way that we automatically look lovingly on God, and from then onwards call him "Abba, Father"? If it does then why do so many baptized people lapse from serving a loving Father? Surely it is because they never really knew him as a personal, loving Father, and we must not be afraid to explore and ask the reason why.

I have met baptized Christians whose primary loyalty to their institution or fellowship is so intense and exhaustive that their relationship with God as a loving Father is diminished, nearly to the point of exclusion. There are Catholics who suffer in this respect, namely that religion supersedes faith, but they are by no means alone in this failing. Margaret, a very convinced Baptist, came to a few of our healing sessions and later confessed:

I believed not so much in a personal God who was the Father of all Christians but in a God who was the exclusive right of Baptists. I became so involved with the little things of our group, the nuts and bolts of our church, that I began to think we could get on without God. He was there when we needed him, but it was more important to be accepted and loved in our fellowship, than it was to know God as a Father who loved us personally. Oh yes, I proclaimed Jesus as my personal Saviour, and God the Father as someone whose personal love for me was indispensable, but they were words which, through repetition, no longer penetrated my mind and heart. I needed healing in order to renew my Christian faith and zeal. It was shattering for me to discover how shallow my faith had become.

Margaret was healed and renewed in the Spirit and has, I am sure, brought with her a spirit of renewal to her local community.

True, the sacrament of baptism puts us right into the centre of Christ's death and resurrection. "You have been taught that when we were baptized in Christ Jesus we were baptized in his death; in other words, when we were baptized we went into the tomb with him and joined him in death, so that as Christ was raised from the dead by the Father's glory, we too might live a new life" (Romans 6:3-4). It is also true that by baptism we are *reconciled* to the Father, and called to live the new life of grace. But we know only too well the effects of sin which remain in our lives even after reconciliation. "I cannot understand my own behaviour. I fail to carry out the things I want to do, and I find myself doing the very things I hate . . . The fact is, I know of nothing good living in me – living, that is, in my unspiritual self – for though the will to do what is good is in me, the performance is not, with the result that instead of doing the good things I want to do, I carry out the sinful things I do not want. When I act against my will, then, it is not my true self doing it, but sin which lives in me" (Romans 7:15, 18-20).

Besides our reconciliation with the Father, which breaks down the barrier that sin puts between us, *we need further and constant healing*. This healing comes to us through the Holy Spirit as his gift "which makes us cry out Abba, Father!" (Romans 8:15). As I have said, we know that not everyone who is baptized has so experienced a personal

91

God as to call God 'Abba, Father', though we all should do because we all receive the Holy Spirit at baptism. It is also true that not every "born-again Christian" remains true to his calling once he has received the Spirit. Sadly, I have met all too many who have been led by the Evil One down the road of self-righteousness and exclusiveness. It is too painful for me to catalogue such incidences, but even in many "born-again" movements I have discerned quite clearly the lack of the presence of the Holy Spirit. *Every Christian, whatever the origins of his calling, needs constant healing*, and the reason quite simply is that the attractions of the world can dim and lessen our awareness and response to God as our loving Father. We all need healing and renewing every day of our lives.

God the Father loves us with a love which never ebbs and flows. It is as unchangeable and unchanging as his own life. Our love is fickle, and sometimes we fail to respond to his love, going our own way in sin just like the Prodigal Son. The main points we learn from this story (Luke 15:11-32), are that while the Father's love remains unchanging and personal for both his sons, it is they who are in need of healing. The younger one needs the healing of repentance: the elder the healing of reconciliation. The sad thing is that many Christians feel that, because they have estranged themselves from God, he has, in consequence, distanced himself from them.

Here is a simple story to illustrate this point. Jerry was the misfit of his family, and as soon as age permitted, he sought his freedom in the "big wide world". He very soon fell on hard times, and developed a severe drink problem. He was referred to me by his doctor, who warned him that if he kept up his drinking habits he would not have long in this world. I soon discovered in Jerry a bitterness towards his family, a self-destructive hatred of himself, and anger towards God who "let" him get into such a state. I talked and prayed with him, and eventually he realized that God was his Father who never ceased loving him. This so affected him as a person that he completely changed his way of life. He was reunited with his family, and developed a proper respect for himself as a person. Today he is an extraordinary minister of Holy Communion in his local church. In his case the three areas of relationship were healed: with God, with his family and within himself. Again I have hundreds of testimonies like Jerry's in my files, but the point I want to stress is that it is essential for us as Christians to remember that *God's love for us is unchanging even when we change for the worse, and forget him* as being of any importance in our lives. We may think we are worthless. God our Father thinks the opposite, especially when we have no one to love us, not even ourselves.

Because God is a loving Father whose relationship with us is personal, intimate, unique and unchangeable, he never ceases to love us. When we sin it is we, not God, who put up the barrier between us. We are always given the grace or opportunity to return to our Father's house, but we have to respond freely to his invitation. "I did not come to call the virtuous," said Jesus, "but sinners to repentance" (Luke 5:32). The mission of Jesus was a mission to sinners to return to their Father's home. His Father, he told us time and again, was a *forgiving God*. Jesus' forgiveness of his executioners, when he hung on the cross, was the last expression and obedient act of a Son who knew that was what his heavenly Father wanted him to do. No sin, not even the murder of his own Son, was outside the scope of God's mercy and forgiveness. "Since God did not spare his own Son, but gave him up to benefit us all, we may be certain, after such a gift, that he will not refuse anything he can give. Could anyone accuse those that God has chosen? When God acquits, could anyone condemn?

Could Christ Jesus? No! He not only died for us – he rose from the dead, and there at God's right hand he stands and pleads for us" (Romans 8:32-34). So many otherwise good Christians fail to live the good life because their memories are haunted by the sins of their past. They believe that in some way, if they are to recover God's love and pardon, they must spend the rest of their lives in penitential acts and prayers. Their sorrows are an acute form of remorse, and a sense of shame lest those around them would know them for what they were. It is, in a sense, the sin of despair.

Mary from Bradford is a typical example of this form of "abandoned soul". Her childhood involved her in acts of incest with her father for which she could never forgive herself. She haunted the church and developed severe bouts of depression. Eventually, when she was on the point of entering a mental institution, she came to one of our healing sessions. I laid her sins side by side against the forgiveness of the Father, and eventually she was healed and learned to forgive both her father and herself. Her bitterness disappeared as well as her hatred of herself and her own body. Her prayer life became one of joy and gratitude, so that the three areas of personal relationship were healed.

Only God can forgive sin, because his love for us overcomes it. We cannot do it on our own, no matter how hard we try. So, belief in a forgiving God is of the essence of our Christian faith and hope. "For I am certain of this: neither death nor life, no angel, no prince, nothing that exists, nothing still to come, not any power, or height or depth, nor any created thing, can ever come between us and the love of God made visible in Christ Jesus our Lord" (Romans 8:38-39). Those who constantly stress the heinousness of sin without emphasizing the limitless mercy and forgiveness of a loving Father, do a grave disservice to the Christian Gospel. Vincent, a long-time friend of mine, was spiritually crippled for years because of a mission given in his school by a preacher who "laid into them" on sex.

> That mission made such an impression on me that for the past forty-five years, I can hear the priest's voice ringing in my ears. I knew then that I had committed sins of sexual abuse against myself, and they were made to sound so terrible that I was convinced God would punish me for them. I had confessed them several times but I could not shake them off my conscience or out of my mind. They so affected my prayer life that my head was always down when I prayed and I could never raise a really sincere word of praise or thanksgiving. God was not so much a loving Father but the Father I had betrayed. I was saturated with guilt feelings which were never far from the surface.

Vincent's healing was a slow process, but he gradually learned to forgive himself because he believed that God his Father had already done so. His case is typical of many who are trapped in the bog of self-condemnation since they limit the mercy of God to their own narrow dimensions.

Only those who have experienced it will ever know the extent of God's forgiveness. This is exemplified by the woman who was a sinner who went to meet Jesus in Simon the Pharisee's house. She wept over Jesus' feet and poured ointment over them. Jesus said to Simon, "I tell you that her sins, her many sins, must have been forgiven her, or she would not have shown such great love. It is the man who is forgiven little who shows little love" (Luke 7:47). In all healing the paramount factor to be kept before people's minds and hearts is that the love and forgiveness of our heavenly Father know no bounds.

No less than the height of heaven over earth
is the greatness of his love for those who fear him;
he takes our sins farther away
than the east is from the west.
As tenderly as a father treats his children,
so God treats those who fear him;
he knows what we are made of,
he remembers we are dust (Psalm 103:11-14).

God is always there loving us, but we are not always there loving him. Love needs two to have a relationship. What is needed on our part is a response to his love through *conversion and repentance*. If sin is abandoning the Father's house, conversion and repentance mean returning to it. Even though repentance and conversion are graces from our Father in Christ — "He wants us home" — and even though God in Christ calls and welcomes the sinner, he does not force his return. He is like the Prodigal Son in the gospel story who, looking at the squalor all around him and the depths to which he has sunk, has to decide himself what he must do, "and he would willingly have filled his belly with the husks the pigs were eating but no one offered him anything. *Then he came to his senses* and said, 'How many of my father's paid servants have more food than they want, and here am I dying of hunger! *I will leave this place* and go to my father and say: *Father, I have sinned against heaven and against you*; I no longer deserve to be called your son; treat me as one of your paid servants.' So he left the place and went back to his father" (Luke 15:16-20).

We know the Father's love which we experience through the Spirit, and so in sorrow yet with expectancy we retrace our steps home. We do not do so in a sense of wounded pride, or anger at letting ourselves, and even our Christian calling, down. Rather we come in sorrow, humbly admitting that we have betrayed the love of a Father who is good beyond our wildest dreams. We recognize that by our deeds and life-style we do not merit God's forgiveness, but, acknowledging our sinfulness, we ask in the name of Jesus Christ our Lord, and in the Power of his Spirit, that we be forgiven – and the end result is always the same. The love relationship is resumed and our life takes on a new dimension and spiritual dialogue.

> "Come now, let us talk this over",
>   says God.
> "Though your sins are like scarlet
> they shall be as white as snow;
> though they are red as crimson,
> they shall be as white as wool" (Isaiah 1:18).

Once we get our relationship right with God, then the other relationships with our neighbour and within ourselves will fall into place. The real test of the sincerity of our repentance will always be whether or not we in turn are ready and *willing to forgive those who have hurt us*. We are hurt in a million different ways and will not be healed of these hurts until we put them all, *one by one*, into the basket of an air balloon and let the Holy Spirit blow them away. In Derry I prayed with a young woman who had lost her boyfriend on Bloody Sunday. She was angry with God, the police, the British army, everyone, because her life had been brought to a tragic halt by the death of the young man she had hoped to marry. Surprisingly enough, she was not bitter, but in her heart she could not forgive those responsible for his death. Gradually, *one by one*, I brought them before her mind, and in one of the most beautiful inner healings I have ever witnessed she forgave them all. Of course the tears flowed, but they were of release and not the sheer emotionalism one would normally expect on such occasions. The healing was gentle and peaceful, and only the few of us near her knew the great gift of mercy that was flowing through her from God her loving Father. Her life has changed through this inner healing and she has matured remarkably. Behind her were twelve years of mourning, and now her life in the future has become one of compassion and hope. We cannot love God as a Father in isolation from the rest of the community. "Anyone who claims to be in light but hates his brother is still in the dark. But anyone who loves his brother is living in the light and need not be afraid of stumbling; unlike the man who hates his brother, and is in the darkness, not knowing where he is going" (1 John 2:9-11). In my ministry of healing I have found that the most powerful way to experience and receive the Father's healing forgiveness is to forgive those who hurt us, and I gave a testimony to this healing power in my own life in the second chapter of this book.

The Gospel of Jesus is full of forgiveness, and he condemned the lack of it far more times than he did sins of the flesh. In the story of the woman taken in adultery it was the need to forgive that he highlighted (John 8:3-11). Mercy and forgiveness, not justice and condemnation, were the hallmarks of his teaching and life. "You have learnt how it was said: You must love your neighbour and hate your enemy. But I say this to you: love your enemies and pray for those who persecute you; in this way you will be sons of your Father in heaven, for he causes his sun to rise on bad men as well as good, and his rain to fall on honest and dishonest men alike" (Matthew 5:43-45). If we want to be sons of the Father, says Jesus, the solution is straightforward and uncomplicated: "If you forgive others their failings, your heavenly Father will forgive you yours; but if you do not forgive others, your Father will not forgive your failings either" (Matthew 6:14-15). Once we really experience God the Father's loving forgiveness for us, then it is impossible for us not to forgive those who hurt us. One does not come before the other, they come together like two sides of a coin. Jesus loved everyone because he was a true Son of the Father. Forgiveness is of the essence of every form of spiritual healing.

In healing I have found that people always fail to be released from their burdens until and unless they forgive their enemies. The hidden bigotry, the denominational distrust, are often laid bare once the Spirit of love starts to open old, hidden wounds in order to heal them. It is a painful but necessary process. Roger, a Presbyterian minister, spelled out the pain of forgiveness.

> I was quite content to fraternize and pray with my Roman Catholic brethren, but deep down even though I admired most of them I still felt they were not Christian. They were not real Bible people, with all this emphasis on the Pope and statues and things. In some weird, inexplicable way, I identified them with nationalism so that already a barrier was erected between us. Then one of my Roman friends' church was bombed and I had to try and understand how he felt. It was a painful process but as we prayed together we realized how far apart we had grown over the years in our denominations, so that when we prayed together, while we were still using the same words in our prayers, they did not mean the same thing to us. We were praying to a Protestant God and a Catholic God. Now we pray to our Father, and as we come closer to Him we discover more areas of healing between and within us both.

Roger said it all.

The most difficult area of healing will always remain *the shedding of our false notions of God*. The Devil has done a wonderful job through those who teach and preach his kingdom of an unqualified fear of hell. We have many advocates of that kind of fear of God. We can have no real relationship as faithful and loving children of God our Father unless we actually live out the life of Jesus Christ his Son, under the inspiration of the Holy Spirit. Many of the healings in my ministry have been *deliverance from fear and guilt* whose roots were deeply intertwined and entangled with false teaching in early childhood, which twisted and stunted the intellectual, spiritual, emotional and even physical growth of the individual. It is for this reason that I shall devote separate chapters to fear and guilt, which have so adversely affected our relationship with God, with each other and within ourselves.

But however hard we try to understand God the Father's love and forgiveness, and attempt to prepare ourselves for our journey home, we will still fall far short of the reality. Our explanations and sorrow for sin will be muffled by the Father's love. "While he was still a long way off, his father saw him and was moved with pity. He ran to the boy, clasped him in his arms and kissed him tenderly" (Luke 15:20-21). The darkness of sin will be lost in the brightness of his love. Our protests that we "no longer deserve to be called your son; treat me as one of your hired servants" (Luke 15:19-20) will be swept aside by the Father who gives the order: "'Quick! Bring out the best robe and put it on him; put a ring on his finger and sandals on his feet. Bring the calf we have been fattening, and kill it; we are going to have a feast, a celebration, because *this son of mine* was dead and has come back to life; he was lost and is found'. And they began to celebrate" (Luke 15:22-24).

Our total healing will be complete only in heaven, but the healing of our relationship with God our Father is not just the forgiving of sin. It turns us outwards towards healing with our neighbour, and inwards towards healing deep within ourselves. The Christian life is a circle of healing love joining us with God the Father and with each other, the centre of which is Christ the wounded healer, and the healing force is the Spirit of love which heals us and makes us one.

8.

The Healing of Friendships

God our Father did not mean us to live alone, or to live for ourselves alone: "It is not good for the man to be alone" (Genesis 2:18). We are part of the human family, and we grow as persons in the world of people through the discovery in them of ourselves and of God. We need other people in order to know who God is, and who we are. People are the mirror of our world, and if we smash it to pieces, or cover it over, then we will die within ourselves, like a plant which withers and dies when it is denied the light necessary for its growth. Christ is the light of, and for, our world. The sad thing in our world is that the mirror, broken by sin, gives such a distorted view of reality that we see only certain parts of it, and never really get the whole picture into focus. People are disorientated in our fragmented community. Broken relationships between nations, religions, social groupings, and even in the tiny unit of the family itself, are shattered as rapidly as the broken windscreen of a car. They do not know who they are any more, or where they belong, or what their destiny and purpose is. We are not at peace within ourselves, or with God, because we are at war with each other. The ministry of healing over the past decade has opened me to a world full of loneliness and heart-ache, of bitterness and frustration, of a seething anger not far below the surface because deep down in their hearts people know this is not the way they should be living in our world, and yet they feel powerless to do anything about it. There is as much need for *healing in the community* today as at any time in my experience.

We cannot live in a world in which we say we love God and love ourselves in a truly Christian way if we exclude everyone else. If we want to grow in the proper love of God, and of ourselves, we need people. Everyone needs the healing support of friends. As soon as he began his public life, Jesus surrounded himself with apostles and disciples with whom he shared his mission, his ideas, his emotions, his time and his friendship. "A man can have no greater love than to lay down his life for his friends. You are my friends, if you do what I command you. I shall not call you servants any more, because a servant does not know his master's business; I shall call you friends because I have made known to you everything I have learnt from my Father. You did not choose me, no, I chose you" (John 15:13-16). He shared his moment of glory of the transfiguration with his three close friends, Peter, James and John (Matthew 17:2-8), and it was to them that he turned for help and healing in his moment of need in the Garden of Gethsemane: "My soul is sorrowful to the point of death, wait here and keep awake" (Mark 14:34). In his need of friends Jesus showed that everyone needs people to help them grow, people with whom they can share their moments of triumph and tragedy.

Jesus was sent into a world of people and lived a life of reconciliation and healing. In studying, imitating and experiencing his life-style we come to an appreciation of what it is to be fully human, fully alive. He wanted to be a friend of everyone, and loved even his enemies, forgiving those who crucified him. He preached and lived a Gospel that "if you love those who love you, what right have you to claim any credit?" (Matthew 5:46). He held that selfish love is of its nature self-destructive. So if we really want to love ourselves in the best sense of the word, then we need to look not only deeply inside ourselves, but outside ourselves as well, so that we can share our love with others and in the process grow and mature as persons.

Time and again in our healing services we encounter people who are locked in on themselves, and are *afraid to reach out to others*. They are like the creature "E.T." in the film of the same name. When he meets his first humans, even though they are only young, innocent children, he is afraid of contact. I have countless examples of this form of inner healing. Jim, a highly intellectual Scot, was afraid to make contact with others at a friendship level.

I met them academically and appreciated their value in their line of expertise, but I cannot say I ever made a deep lasting friendship with any of them. I suppose I was afraid of reaching out to them because of the unknown consequences involved, so it was better to keep everything on the sure foundation of business. This attitude carried over into my ordinary, everyday life with my wife and family. I had to be sure I was not going to be hurt by anyone, so I stayed behind the guarded frontier of my own life and personal sanctuary. Until I was healed, I never knew how much I missed in life, and how lonely I had become.

Today Jim has matured in a beautiful way, because maturity has nothing to do with age but with our response to experiences in life. He is joyful, one of the characteristics of those who receive the Holy Spirit, and are "released". He is not "gushing" or "hail fellow well met", but a truly sincere person whose Christian friendship I value. Like many others who are healed, he assists our healing team whenever we visit his area, and we are never far from each other's thoughts and prayers.

We live in a world which is full of lonely people who are sad and so tense.inside, that they feel "all knotted up". They want to cry out for the help of friends, but the words freeze on their lips, because they don't want their walls of

Jericho to come tumbling down. "Business as usual" is their motto, even though deep down in their hearts they want to run away from it all. They may have every materialistic comfort money can buy, and yet they live in a desert of their own fashioning. I have discerned that many of these people weep inside their tears of the spirit and soul, and it is in the recognition of this loneliness that very often the process of "healing of the person" begins. It is mainly for this reason that the *gift of discernment* is so essential to the ministry of healing. Time and again when I have spoken gently to people about the loneliness within them, and its causes, they are amazed that anyone knows how they feel deep inside. This gives them the confidence, spiritually and psychologically, to reach out for God's help in human form, and eventually when I have ministered to them they are able to reach out to others. *The inner healing which releases them to others is very similar, and as sensitive as the release of "loving yourself as God wants you to".* The human person is a very fragile plant which withers easily in the wrong temperature, or under someone's bruising touch. The value of the "healing touch" is a subject I shall develop later in this book.

Loving someone else is not only the most attractive and necessary element in our human personality, but also the most dangerous. Some people who consider themselves called to the healing ministry talk far too quickly and lightly about "going out in love" to other people, seeing this as a remedy for everyone. We have to see other people, and the world, through their own frightened eyes, much as E.T. looked at the young children who later became his friends. To make a real attempt at friendship is to take a leap into the unknown, and life is a continuing journey of exploration and discovery of self in other people. Many people never make this leap.

Paddy, a big, silent Irishman living in England, was so

locked in on himself that he constantly suffered severe bouts of depression. No amount of psychiatric or medical treatment seemed to help him. In fact it made him worse. He was a single man, whose brothers and sisters pined for his recovery, and prayed that he would make some form of contact with them or with anyone else, but Paddy seemed oblivious to their language of love, or their concern. He was, to all intents and purposes, a zombie. When he first came for healing, I prayed that his inner fears would be released. I did not lay hands on him as I did not feel called to do so. After the healing prayer he looked the same on the outside as before, and yet I discerned that his healing had begun. He came back again to another healing session a few months later, with his brothers and sisters. This time I felt called to lay hands on him, very gently without words, and after a minute or so I felt the coldness of his fear disappear. At the next healing session I blessed the hands of his brothers and sisters, and asked them to lay their hands very gently and lovingly on Paddy. After about half an hour I noticed the frightened look leave his eyes, and saw his hands reach out very slowly and furtively towards his family. Today Paddy is growing as a person, and when he laughs there is no tension or anxiety in him but relief and a sense of freedom. *God used his family to heal him, and through them he is learning to reach out to other people.* There are times when depression returns, but it is becoming less frequent, less intense and for much shorter periods. Soon it will disappear altogether. Through his family and friends he is becoming the healthy person that God his Father wants him to be. The medical profession said there was no cure for him, and even the clergy held firmly to the belief that his mental state was a cross that he and his family would always have to bear. God the loving Father, who wants to heal his children, proved them wrong.

Once we reach out in love and trusting friendship to

another, we will never be the same person as before. Love cannot stand still. Each encounter in which we leave ourselves open in trust to another, is either for our healing or our hurt. There is no painless way of loving, no other way of healing and growing. Only those who have been hurt by friends and those closest to them in the family, know and appreciate the inner healing power of friendship. There will be times when people hurt us, and we will be tempted to withdraw behind the safety of the barriers of our own self-defence. It is at times like these that the words of St Paul help us: "Christ is the peace between us . . . he has broken down the barrier . . . In his own person he killed the hostility . . . Through him, both of us have in the one Spirit our way to come to the Father" (Ephesians 2:14,17,18). If Christ's peace is in us then nothing that anyone does to us can disturb our inner peace.

A word of caution in healing for those who are withdrawn, but who like Paddy have discovered the presence of God's love within themselves, and so are able to begin to reach out to people who love them for themselves. They are like children in a whole new, wonderful, yet strange, world, and we must treat them with the greatest sensitivity and gentleness. They are like rabbits playing in a field, which at the slightest disturbance will head for the safety of their burrow. Once they discover a friend in another person, then that person will lead them gently to another and so on, until eventually all fear and apprehension will disappear.

It is a slow healing process, and each of us has to go through it time and again to recover our own lost ground whenever a friend whom we love dearly betrays our trust. It was so with Jesus and his friends, the Apostles. When we offer friendship we offer ourselves, and in such a gesture there is always a danger of rejection. Those who have been rejected and then healed are usually the best ministers of this form of healing. *In no way must we presume that because a person is withdrawn the source of such withdrawal is some unforgiven sin.* Such treatment without due discernment is self-righteous, and gravely harmful. I have had to minister in repairing such damage in countless cases, and regard those who act in such a way as to cause this harm as the very people who themselves need healing.

When we stand before people as their friends we are like Christ who stands outside Lazarus' tomb and bids him to come forth. Our caring and love must be in the same vein as that of the Lord Jesus. Our love for people heals and helps them to love themselves, and it is wonderful that God the Father in Christ uses us to heal his wounded world since we are our brothers' keepers. Even though God alone can bring them to wholeness, nevertheless we as loving Christians are his invitation to them to open their minds, hearts and persons through our visible caring and sharing of their lives. We are God's mirror for other people, so that in our eyes they can see their value as another loving human person. They want to touch the God they see in us and yet they are terrified of contact. "While he was talking, a shining cloud came over them and a voice from the cloud said 'This is my own dear Son, with whom I am pleased – listen to him!' When the disciples heard the voice they were so terrified that they threw themselves face downwards on the ground. Jesus came to them and touched them. 'Get up', he said. 'Don't be afraid!' So they looked up and saw no one there but Jesus" (Matthew 17:5-8).

People grow through the genuine selfless love of another human being. They have had a surfeit of systems, ideologies and empty talk about "love". They desperately want to see love in action, in a person. They want to hear, see, touch, be in the presence of, someone who loves them for themselves, "*for God's Holy Spirit, God's gift, does not want you to be afraid of people, but* to be wise and strong, and *to love them and to enjoy being with them*" (2 Timothy 1:7). And so once they are healed by God's love, and assisted in their lives by our caring for them, they have to make their way into the world. Generally, it seems to me that the best advice to give to people who are healed of their fear of making friends, is to start gradually with those whom they can trust, someone with a great deal of patience and compassion. Because the friend understands them as they are, they will try to understand him as he is. Soon the healed ones will realize, as they venture out further into the sea of friendship, that it has many levels, depths and shallows with perilous rocks. There will be hurt, but where there is pain there will also be healing and growth. The main thing is that they remain open to friendship, while on the other hand allowing no one to disturb that inner peace of the Holy Spirit which they have received. It is the oxygen they need to breathe for life. Once they have known inner peace and valued it, they can assess friendships for their true value. They will learn that friendship is essentially a giving and sharing. As they grow in Christian love they will be able to share more, but to go "over the top" in loving someone is just not spiritually true and is emotionally dangerous. It is expecting far too much of fallen human nature, however deeply healed it may be.

We live in a world under the shadow of sin. Selfless, caring, healing love is such a rare commodity that often when we reach out in genuine friendship to another, we will be rebuffed and driven back in on ourselves. It is then that we need the healing of Christ who knew rejection by friends at first-hand. Our so-called Christian world, even in the closed circuit of religious communities, is not ready to live the Christian ethic to the full. I have found that *hurtful relationships are the most destroying factor of inner peace and the human personality*. The reason friendship, or reaching out to others, ends in failure is because we tend to manipulate and possess other people for our own selfish ends. A true friendship can only grow by letting the other person be "other" in his freedom and love, just as God allows us to be free and "other" to him. Each person is a mystery in himself, and it will take a lifetime discovering more and more about the "other" even though it is through others that we get to know ourselves. This is what *a healing, Christian community is all about: letting each one be different and be uniquely himself.* This community sharing is a very valuable avenue of healing and is not unlike group therapy. The tragedy with so many prayer groups is that they fail to go deeper into an understanding of each other, and so remain on the periphery of their awareness of each member of the group as unique, as someone who is for our healing as we are for theirs. The ministry of one who is always healing in a group, but never asks for healing, is in my opinion very suspect.

People are damaged within themselves, and are unable to shake off the shadows of past events which cloud their openness to others. These events cripple them emotionally and psychologically, and until they are healed they cannot live a full and free Christian life. Arthur was a misfit in his large family. All his brothers and sisters did well at school, in business and in their personal lives.

"No one took any notice of me," said Arthur, "so I did everything contrary to their respectable way of acting. I deliberately chose the wrong type of companions, gambled and drank excessively, and eventually got into trouble with the police for minor breaches of the peace. In fact, I wanted to be caught just like a runaway dog. I hated my family, and had a grudge against the world. I never returned home because I would not know where to start a conversation with them. It is all such a mess. I suppose they hope that the black sheep of the family is dead and buried in some distant land. And yet there are times when I lie awake at night and wonder where they are, and what they are doing."

His healing process did not start with his alcoholism, or his bouts of anger with his family and society. I soon discerned that Arthur did not love himself, and that is where I started. After just two pretty short healing sessions he saw his life and events much more clearly, and allowed God the Father into his life. He returned to his prayer life and his home, and today normal, human relationships are restored between him and his brothers and sisters. Because he is restored fully to his own family he is able to relate to other people much more easily and deeply.

All human relationships, to be of true value and growth, *are rooted in God's love for us*, and as a consequence our love for him flows out to other people. When we love other people because we see God in them, then our love flows through us back to God. What I am saying in simple terms is that all human relationships must have a "God dimension" to them if they are for our healing and growth, just as we cannot love God if we do not love our neighbour. The truth which is basic to healing, is that only God can love fully in me and that he needs me to love him, so that together we can love the world and people. "You must love the Lord your God with all your heart, with all your soul and with all your mind," said Jesus, "and you must love your neighbour as yourself" (Matthew 22:37-39). Our love has to be *total*. Once we exclude anyone from our friendship then our love of ourselves, and of God, is to that extent diminished. I have many case histories to illustrate this point, and I have only to look inside my own life to see how just one bitter feeling was crippling my attitude towards God, my neighbour and myself.

Marriage is a typical example too of how human relationships can destroy people. Marriages flounder so often on the rocks of the dominant, even the domineering partner, becoming the "we" of the partnership. Where marriage is not true sharing then the prospects of healing are very much reduced. Our chauvinist society has done as much to damage people in their married relationship as the exaggerated female liberation movement. Love is not a *quid pro quo*, because a "what's in it for me?" approach militates against sharing. Marriage, as marriage, can only be healed when *both parties* are prepared to change, and to be open to each other because both form a unity. They need to see life as an adventure not knowing what each day brings. Marriage is not a comfortable, static institution, but a dynamic challenge to grow which both need to accept if there is to be true inner peace and growth for both husband and wife. I could quote hundreds of cases where both parties have been healed, and the marriage relationship has changed and grown, but this has never happened where one party is self-righteous and possessive. The healing of marriage, like all other forms of inner healing, is intimately and essentially linked with "healing of memories". There is a whole area of healing within marriages which needs prayer, investigation and guidelines from the churches.

Tom helps us to focus on the healing needed in marriage.

I loved Mary deeply, and at the beginning we were very happy together. I got lost in my business, she got lost in the children, until we lost sight of each other as "husband and wife". The children had grown up and left home. We had grown apart. We tried everything, marriage guidance, the lot, but it was of little use. Then one day we both came to your healing session, and it was as if God was touching us both, and encouraging us to make a fresh start. We have done so, and now in a beautiful sense God is using us to heal each other. He shows us areas of each other's personality which we have never discovered before. It is an on-going process, but we know that God healed us and that only he could.

Some married couples who came to our healing sessions were not healed, because deep down in their minds and hearts they were not prepared to change their attitudes, and wanted the other partner to do all the changing! What is needed is a "conversion", a complete change of heart, which unfortunately is seen by them as the destruction of their personality. If love is a sharing then it is also a changing and a growing.

There is another form of division in human relationships, and that is between the Christian churches. Despite being heavily involved for over a decade in the search for peace and reconciliation in Northern Ireland, I still continue to be saddened by the division between the churches, not only in that beleaguered land, but also here in England. A few months ago a Free Church friend of mine for many years, told me how surprised he was that while I was a Christian I still remained a Roman Catholic Priest. He needed healing of his bigotry and ignorance!! There is a massive healing to be done in many people of different denominations, who so distrust each other that they are more aware of what divides rather than what unites them. I could fill a book with stories of quite extraordinary inner healings and changes of attitude which I have experienced at first hand at our meetings in England as well as in Northern Ireland. At one of our healing sessions in Sheffield I discerned a very deep, angry sense of hostility from a member of the congregation. In my heart I prayed for her release from whatever was binding her. Later I felt moved to go and quietly ask her, "Why do you hate me?" She replied immediately and spontaneously: "Because you are a Catholic Priest and I have been brought up to hate you." Poor Elizabeth was confused when she saw the Lord was using me as the minister of his healing. She did not know what to believe, as a lot of her preconceived judgements were being challenged by what she saw. Today she is healed even though she has had to face the anger of her parents at her change of attitude and heart. All Christian denominations are guilty of bigotry and sectarianism, and only the Lord himself can heal the sad, crippling divisions between the churches. Much is being done in this area of healing but a great deal more has yet to be achieved.

There are many other areas of inner healing between people, which in a future time and book I shall develop. Suffice it here to say that healing of relationships between persons is one of the most difficult and sensitive areas of healing.

While remaining open to being misunderstood I believe that all forms of physical healing are much easier and more glamorous than the inner healing of human relationships. Our world is so contaminated by the pollution of prejudice, power and selfishness that it is well-nigh impossible to breathe the pure air of friendship as God intended we should. It is for this reason that we need to return time and again for inner healing, so that we may rediscover "who is my neighbour", and in Christ love him.

9.

Learning to Love Yourself and Be Healed

Most social workers agree that the greatest single cause of unhappiness, loneliness and frustration among people, is that they do not love themselves. This seems a strange assertion when the opposite would seem to be true in a very sophisticated, computerized, materialistic world, where people are obsessed with themselves and their own interests. This is not loving themselves in the way they should, as much as projecting an image which the world demands as acceptable. It is a sham "me" which they "love", and they know it.

Peter from Edinburgh is someone who typifies the sham people with whom we rub shoulders in our everyday world, but never come to know because they are afraid to be, and to love, themselves.

All my life I have felt that I was living an unreal life. I never got to know the real "me" because those around me never encouraged me to be myself. My father wanted me to be a "chip off the old block", a success story, and so I was forced to study for my school exams even during holiday time. There was a pattern of behaviour in my home to which I had to conform for peace's sake. I never really made friends at school, and later on I subconsciously used people for my own advantage. I went into business, and did reasonably well because people around me lived a sham, and I was used to counterfeit living by then. In fact I was so good at it, and

115

could see its immediate benefits, that there was no urgency or desire to seek reality. I married, and had a fairly happy family life, until I noticed that I too was manipulating my children at an early age, into becoming adroit at the game of "sham" or "you'll never know the real me". Now for me the game is up and I realize that if I am to make anything of my life I must get to know the real me. I am unhappy, trying desperately to face myself, and wondering in a rather frightened way how much damage I have done to my children.

I had four long healing sessions with Peter, and there were times when he became quite abusive with me, and would take himself off rather defiantly to his sham world. But today he is much improved. He is beginning to accept himself, make true friends, and pray in a way which shows that he is gradually letting the light of the Father's love shine on his life. He is well on his way to recovery along the path of self-discovery and self-appreciation.

Peter is typical of so many hundreds I meet in the healing ministry. The world is full of shams and they, too, penetrate the world of inner healing. They think they know what they want, but because they do not really love themselves as they should, they cannot possibly love God our Father as they should, and do not leave it to him. They put up their hands for healings of their own choice, but what they are asking for is not what they really need. During healing sessions I always insist on using the gift of discernment, going only to minister to those to whom the Spirit directs me. I am not worried by this selective approach, because it is only the Spirit who heals, and he will guide me. There are "sham" healers for "sham" illnesses, and these people seem happy in the role-playing and financial gain or comfort which usually follow!

Why should people love themselves? The answer is

simple: because God the Father made them, and he loves what he has made. We may not love ourselves, but that is because our vision is limited to the "mirror on the wall", whereas God reads the heart. God loves us. If we do not love ourselves, or in other words appreciate who we are and what is our purpose in life, then we are really saying to God, "I am sorry that you made me this way". "Does the clay say to its fashioner, 'What are you making?' does the thing he shaped say, 'You have no skill?' Woe to him who says to a father, 'What have you begotten?' or to a woman, 'To what have you given birth?'" (Isaiah 45:9-10). So the person who does not love himself says, "I am going to make up a new me that I can 'love', and which other people will respect". The sham game has begun. It is one of the most difficult barriers to break through in healing, and the pain involved is quite soul-searing, as the bandages of self-deception are peeled off the mummified figure in the hope that there is some personal life and identity left. This form of inner healing of the true self is the most rewarding, and one of the principal channels of our healing ministry.

If you do not know and love yourself for who and what you are, then how can you love God? You find no reason in your real self for loving him, so at best in your sham world he becomes the God of religious comfort who blesses you abundantly with this world's goods as a fore-taste of the next, or at worst a vicious God who is responsible for all your misfortunes. If you do not love yourself deep down within yourself, then you cannot love anyone else in the same way. We are asked to forgive our neighbour only as we forgive ourselves, but if we do not forgive the real self and allow it to emerge, then we do not forgive our neighbour his real self, so he too is condemned to play the "sham". Our attitude towards others is conditioned by our attitude to ourselves. Jesus said "You must love the Lord your God with all your heart, with all your soul, and with all your mind. This is the greatest and first commandment. The second resembles it: You must love your neighbour as yourself" (Matthew 2:37-39). We can only love God and our neighbour as much as we love our real selves. If we love anyone *more* than ourselves then we do not really love ourselves as we should. The more we truly love ourselves, the more we will love God and our neighbour, which will in turn help us to love ourselves at a deeper level.

John was very withdrawn the first time he came to one of our healing sessions. He was afraid of any physical contact, even a warm handshake. This, as he explained to me, was a sign of something deeper.

> I never really knew my parents who were afraid to show any form of affection to each other, or to us as children. I never made *contact* with them or my brothers in any way. At school I could have pretended to reach out to my colleagues but I was afraid of rejection. If they rejected me then my whole life would be shattered, so today I live alone within myself, afraid to look at myself lest I too reject what I discover.

John's healing began as, in prayer, we helped him, not only to look at himself, his parents and family life, but at his relationship with God. The thing he found hardest to accept, but yet which was the source of his healing, was that God was his Father who had never stopped loving him and never would. It opened up a whole new life and world to him. It was like teaching a baby how to walk, or to talk the new language of love. John is healed now and is very happily married. He feels "wobbly" at times, but he knows these sessions of withdrawal will pass because he is a person who knows who he is, and what his worth is to God, to others and above all to himself.

It is God the Father's love which heals. What he offers is

not medicine, psychiatry, or counselling, but the warmth of his own Spirit within us. "Your body, you know, is the temple of the Holy Spirit, who is in you since you received him from God" (1 Corinthians 6:19). All I try to do in the healing ministry is to encourage "sham" people to trust themselves to the Lord, and to allow themselves to be soaked in his love. The God who made them can remould them so that they will achieve their fulfilment, purpose and healthy happiness in life.

Invariably I have found this process to be a gentle one, once the person agrees to be healed and to be changed. This moment of decision is like the "Yes" of conception and pain of birth all rolled into one. The release that follows is one of the most beautiful experiences in inner healing, like a rainbow spanning the sky as the gentle rain of tears brings new life to a parched soul. Since it is God alone who always heals, the approach in healing is always one of caring silence rather than a whole lot of words. In the healing of "people becoming themselves", this silence, especially, is one of sensitivity and patience which is much more necessary than in any other form of healing. It is pointless, in fact harmful, to keep urging them strongly and loudly to "love" themselves. To do so is a sign of lack of faith in the "healer", who alone is God and whose love heals.

In the process of letting God's light shine on their lives there is a period of pain, and many have falsely interpreted this as a sign of the need for deliverance. Let me give you an example. Betty came to a healing session, during which she was beginning to experience God the Father's caring love for her. She did not know how to deal with this new element entering her life, and she became confused. Those around "discerned" an evil spirit, and started prayers for her deliverance. These were quite wrong and so frightened her that she was driven in on herself. It took her months to return to another healing session. What she needed was to be surrounded by people who loved and experienced God as a Father. In this warm community she became aware of that love, not only in others, but was beginning to experience it within herself. Through this community of love Betty started "defrosting", so that she could become a real person whom she knew God loved. We were merely the repairers of the broken fuse, or the ones who turned on the switch, but the inner light came from the Holy Spirit. I have heard people so anxious to heal others and help them to experience the love of God within themselves, that they overstress the human, affectionate side of the healing. They keep on saying, "I love you, I love you", or words from the Bible which tell of God's love, instead of just being there, with perhaps a gentle touch of the hand on the head, and the use of the word "peace" in a very warm, soft, soothing tone. Leave the healing to God. I am very much opposed to long embraces, which often stress the emotional need of the "healer" rather than any healing coming from him or her. The danger is that the "healing" will stay at the human level, and not penetrate deep into the inner being of the lonely person. Discernment will show us how we should act so as to be a help rather than a hindrance to God's healing work, in the hyper-sensitive area of a person who needs healing so that he can love himself.

Deep within us there is a power to love ourselves in some way as God loves us, and as we should love ourselves. Only God can make us aware of it, and once we have discovered this power of rare brightness then everything is seen in a new light. The Devil does not want us to have it, and does everything in his power to prevent us searching for it or finding it. We are afraid of what we might discover deep inside ourselves, and so block off the deep areas within us, and live a superficial form of life afraid of the devils within us, whereas it is God whom we have locked up. In the process we have become prisoners locked in on ourselves.

Betty was released by the Spirit of the Risen Jesus. Like Lazarus in the gospel she came forth from the tomb of self to live a new life. Jesus came to "set captives free" (Isaiah 61-1) so that they could be themselves as God wanted them to be, and to lead the Good Life. This is what I understand by being "released in the Spirit". The prison bars of self cannot contain the Holy Spirit, who makes us want to fly as eagles in God's world. Our deep inner self, the self that we want to see grow within us, will emerge so that we are "born again" through the Spirit's power to proclaim the Lordship of Christ and the loving Fatherhood of God. The new life has begun much as a chicken breaking through the shell that encloses it, and the Easter life of Christ shines forth in a person healed to live as God intended we should. Betty made new friends, saw her old friends in a different, more positively loving way, and her life has completely changed. She is a much more joyful person, and lives at a level of serenity deep within herself. Her healing was within her, the healing of the Holy Spirit.

Betty was typical of many people who find it hard to love themselves, and they require the most sensitive Christian healing, which can only come from those who have known the well of loneliness. So we encourage people like Betty to help us in our healing ministry of encouraging people to undertake the search for the discovery of their true selves. We will pray with them, not minimizing the task before them, because they need to believe and trust that God will help them, and that their search will be successful. John is another of many who have been helped through the healing ministry of our community: "When I came first to you," he said, "I was scared stiff. I knew I had to change because my life was so dark and meaningless. Yet I was afraid to change. I needed your hand to help me in the beginning, but deep down within myself I knew that sometime I had to let go of your hand, and walk on my own. I had to trust myself step by step, and at times I felt like turning back, but there was a light ahead and I knew I must find it myself. When I did it, it was only then that I realized what you meant when you were talking about God loving us as we are. Before that it was meaningless jargon to me."

The more fully we accept ourselves, warts and all, the easier we will find change. Everyone who wants healing needs to be changed. This change does not generally happen overnight, and it is in the post-natal care of "new Christians" that we can play a major role. We have to be patient with them and they with themselves. May, from York, came to one of our healing services and proclaimed to all her friends that she was completely healed, and now loved herself through the Holy Spirit which she felt within her, but I discerned that she was only partly healed. She was soon back to self-doubt and self-hatred. However, at the next healing service she was patient with God, and allowed him to work at his own speed. She was then totally healed of her lack of self-love. And not only of that: she was also healed of the asthma from which she had suffered for many years. A lot of damage has been done by attempting too much too soon. Change, like growth, is usually a slow and painful process because we groan and find it a burden "being still in this tent", but success is assured because we have been "given the pledge of the Spirit" (2 Corinthians: 5:4-5).

In our search for ourselves we will discover the parts within us which we have damaged in previous years. We have to learn to look kindly on them, knowing that God is our merciful Father who forgives us. *Whatever we find repulsive is already redeemed.* Our feeling should be one of gratitude that God's never-changing love has been with us all through the years, and that whatever has been in our lives is already redeemed. This aspect of inner healing of our damaged self is most important, and should neither be glossed over nor over-exaggerated. The past is part of us, and we need to heal and soothe its painful memories. The healing of memories is an integral part of learning to love yourself, and I shall deal with it later in more detail. We are damaged people however much we are healed, and damaged people we will remain until the final healing in heaven, when we will be totally healed of all those aspects of our person which still need healing. God will piece together the fragments of our life, and give to each part its full meaning. One of the most beautiful aspects of inner healing is the way those who are healed learn to live one day at a time, in complete trust in God the Father, who provides for all their needs.

I have stressed, and I think rightly so, that inner healing especially comes from God alone, and have said little of the part we have to play in the healing ministry, other than being "defrosters" or "switchers-on of light". Yet our loving contact with others has a very powerful healing effect, in that it helps people to move towards a truer sense of worth in their own eyes. They know, sense, that we are there as *friends* who want to help them, and who will be patient enough to remain there until they want to help themselves. It is a love which liberates and is never possessive, wanting nothing for itself but the good of the other person. An example illustrates my point. For two years Arnold came to our Masses for inner healing, but they seemed to make no impression on him. I urged everyone to pray for him, but I warned them to carry on as "normal" when they met him outside these sessions. I did not want him pressurized, as I have seen so many people descended on by "healers" looking for instant results. One day I discerned in faith that now was the time to approach him. I did so very quietly, laid my hands on his head without words, and he said, "I didn't want anyone near me laying hands on me or praying over me until I was ready. Today I came to Mass praying that you would come and lay your hands on me, because deep down in my heart I was crying out for healing." He was one of the few whom I have witnessed as being completely healed of lack of love for himself at one session. He is now a power-house of prayer for our group ministry healing, especially of people who do not love themselves, because he appreciates what other people suffer. He has been through the valley of darkness himself.

The healing of *being there* for others is most important to all forms of healing. When people do not love themselves then we show that we love them just by being there. The number of people who have learned to love themselves in our healing services is in proportion to the deep prayer and love of the community. When we rid ourselves of our preoccupation with our own needs, or even our selfish desire to "see" the person healed, and concentrate rather on the love of God our Father, leaving it to him to re-create a sense of purpose and self-love in the person to be healed, then we create the best possible atmosphere in which such a healing can take place. It is a loving community which encourages someone not only to walk in the light of God's love, but walks in it with him. If only parishes were true healing communities, then the despairing and lonely would flock to them to be healed, and the healing love of God our Father would be proclaimed.

The healing community at peace within itself shows in clear terms the love of God made visible in people. Those who have no love for themselves will be attracted by its warmth and come in from the cold. I know hundreds of people who have been released by the Spirit to love themselves, even people who thought beforehand that they had already been released. The awareness of a loving God which is tangible at these healing sessions, was the action which turned on the switch, and allowed people so to relax that God's healing love for them came shining through. Communities have to be taught, and to learn, how to be sensitively and *creatively silent* so that the Spirit may move without let or hindrance among his people. The community element is vital in every form of healing, but in none more so than the "releasing" of people to be themselves. When a person has been "released" or healed in order to love himself properly, then his whole life changes. He will need the healing of memories, the gift of forgiveness of those who have injured him as a person, especially the gift of forgiving himself. A whole new life stretches before him. Listen again to Peter:

When I realized that God loved me, and this is what really mattered in life, I had to return in memory and forgive my father. He is long since dead but now I feel sorry for him and for how much he missed. If only we had the chance over again perhaps things would be different, but the past is dead, and I leave it to God's mercy. I hurt so many people by my selfishness, especially my wife and family, but now I make amends not by looking back but by living each day to the full, and what a challenge that is.

The loving of oneself adjusts our relationship with God and our neighbour. They are the axis on which a person moves and grows. Psychiatrists and sociologists hold that the average person lives at a tenth of his potential. There are many people who go to church regularly who never realize, or live out as fully as they could, the Christian life. Their lack of Christian growth has always saddened me. There seems no way of getting through to them, and they are the Church's "walking dead". The invitation to live the Christian life came when God the Father sent his only Son on earth in human form. We have to respond freely to that invitation. The Lord reminds us: "Look, I am standing at the door knocking. If one of you hears me calling and opens the door, I will come in to share his meal, side by side with him" (Revelation 3:20). The door to our heart and person can only be opened from the inside. We hold the key. May God send his Spirit upon us to give us the courage and vision to open the door that leads to health and life.

10.

The Faith That Makes You Whole

The Faith of the One who wants to be Healed

Time and again Jesus told his followers it was faith that made people whole, which healed them. What exactly did he mean? There are countless cases of healing in the gospel, where Jesus seems quite clearly to make healing dependent on the faith of those who looked for healing. When he went to his home town of Nazareth, "he could work no miracles there, though he cured a few sick people by laying his hands on them. He was amazed at their lack of faith" (Mark 6:5-6). When confronted with the opposite extreme, the total faith of the centurion, he healed his servant, even at a distance. "'I tell you solemnly,' said Jesus, 'nowhere in Israel have I found faith like this'. And to the centurion, Jesus said, 'Go back, then; you have believed, so let this be done for you'. And the servant was cured at that moment" (Matthew 8:10,13).

The Jews who were of his own religion did not have enough faith on which Jesus could base his healing power, but the foreign pagan Roman soldier had faith of such a strong kind that Jesus was astonished at it. The Jews believed, or should have done, in God as a Father who could and did heal. The centurion, with his idols and false gods, would not have been expected to have such faith. What exactly did Jesus mean by faith which heals? Was it the faith of the centurion which in the final analysis tipped the scales of healing? Does it mean that there can be no healing where there is no faith in the person who needs to be healed? It would seem so, not only from the juxtaposition of these two stories, but from the whole tenor of the gospels which appear to link healing and the personal faith of the one to be healed. Yet the relationship of faith to healing is not as easy, or as inevitably causally linked, as many people, especially fundamentalist Pentecostals, hold. They insist that if no healing takes place then it is the fault of the person who wants to be healed in having no faith, or at least not sufficient for the healing to be accomplished. I have seen the damage that such a narrow concept of faith and the limiting of God's love as a Father has done in hundreds of people's lives. Mary is a case in point. She has been a paraplegic for many years, and was very bitter when I first met her.

"I have been told by countless Christian ministers of healing that if I had enough faith I could get out of this wheelchair and walk. Oh my God – how I want to, and I just can't. If faith is a gift from God then why doesn't he give this gift of faith to me, so that I can believe enough to be healed? I believe God is punishing me for my sins and that is why I am rotting my life away here in this wheelchair."

What right has anyone to say so categorically that Mary had no faith? Who are we to judge who has faith and who has not? Perhaps a far greater inner healing took place in Mary's life than in the lives of many of her so-called Christian healers, many of whom shouted, quite hysterically, at her to get up and walk. Mary was not healed of her physical illness, but through a period of our praying together she now rests in peace in the Lord, and is able to use her illness much more positively and creatively than many people who have been physically healed. Of course, personal faith helps in the healing, because then we allow God our Father to accomplish through Christ his work of healing in us. Lack of faith is, or can be, a hindrance, when we positively block God's healing power. If faith on our part were the main and indispensable element in healing, then why is it that "born-again Christians" suffer just as much illness as people who have no claims of faith?

We still have to attempt to understand Jesus' statement "Your faith has made you whole" (Luke 7:50). Can our faith actually heal us, and what part does God play in our healing? I believe that there is more to healing than the personal faith of the person wanting to be healed. Even though I need to have faith that God can heal me so as not to put an obstacle in the path of his healing power, nevertheless it is God alone who heals through Christ. *My faith does not heal me.* My faith means that I believe that *God alone has the love and the power to heal, and that healing is ordinary to him.* For over two years I ministered with a group to John, but for some reason he did not appear to receive any healing. Helen, his wife, takes up the story: "John could not believe in his heart that God really wanted to heal him of his depression, worries and anxieties. He felt they were part of the punishment due to him for his sins. Then in one healing session, instead of praying for his healing of depression we prayed that he would become open to the Spirit through the removal of his false attitude to his sins, and a God who seeks vengeance. Within seconds we could visibly see God at work healing him and releasing him from the anxieties that had kept him bound for years." If in the ministry of healing I am led to pray for someone's healing that does not happen then the fault could well lie with me, because I have not known all the circumstances properly, and have used faulty discernment. I cannot, with the deepest faith, possibly unravel the mind and mystery of God. *I cannot say it is because the person to be healed has no faith.*

I remember a few years ago being asked to pray for the

physical healing of a dear, personal friend and great evangelist, David Watson. I prayed for guidance and did not feel called to pray for his physical healing. Instead I prayed for deep, inner peace and resignation for David, strength for his wife Anne, and a firm faith for his followers that they would understand the shock of his death. A few of his over-zealous colleagues chided me for my lack of faith, but I can only pray for what I believe the Lord is calling me to do. Even then I may not be praying for the right thing. God the Father always loves the person for whom I am praying, wants to heal him, but in the way that only he, God, knows is ultimately best for him as a person. David died in great peace. Did that prove me right and the others wrong? Such language is an insult to our loving, healing God.

When I have done all I can in the prayer of faith, then I must *leave the result to God*. Whatever happens, my faith in God is never in question, but my own interpretation or discernment of his will certainly is. I am very hesitant, in my ministry, to say to anyone that they are healed, however anxiously they clamour for me to do so. The temptation is there, but the consequences are catastrophic, both for the person concerned, and for his belief in a healing God. However, there are times when I have no doubt that a person is healed, and in such a way that I have a duty to proclaim it. I have often, almost invariably, found that inner healing occurs before any manifestation of physical healing.

But to return to the faith of the person who asks to be healed, rather than to the faith of the minister of healing. What quality must it have, or can it be dispensed with altogether? Catholics as a rule believe that healings, especially physical, are the exception rather than the rule, and are confined to very holy places like Lourdes or Fatima, or restricted to holy people like the Saints, or

Padre Pio, who will probably be proclaimed one. Their physical sufferings are looked upon as so completely identified with the cross of Jesus, and the Christian way of life, that they feel guilty about asking for healing. Despite their great faith in other matters, and I have myself benefited from it, there must be many Catholics who are not healed because they believe it is right for them to suffer. However, strange things happen to them: I was at one healing session earlier this year and Michael, a Catholic, who could hardly be described as Gospel-greedy, said to himself, "God, I have been suffering with a pain in my side for years. Now, if you really want this priest to heal me, then let him do so without touching me." I never went near Michael, and he was healed instantly of his intestinal pain. Recently I have seen him at some of our Parish Masses for inner healing. Was he healed so that he could believe? I just do not know, but I could quote many similar cases in my healing ministry over the past few years. Does God see the grain of mustard seed of faith hidden from human perception and discernment?

Lack of faith in the person to be healed can be a real obstacle to healing when he definitely does not want to be healed. God gave us a free will, and so we can reject or neglect the gift of faith, and he respects our freedom to do so. He heals us only for some good purpose, and despite some stories which I have been told to the contrary, I have never known one single case in my own healing ministry where someone has been healed, physically, emotionally or spiritually, against his will. I know of hundreds of cases where the person's faith was increased because of their experience.

Here are just a few of the thousand and one attitudes which are *obstacles to healing*:

1. Self-centredness rather than God-centredness. This attitude manifests itself in an over-indulgence of self-pity.
2. Cynicism of the whole healing movement.
3. Despair of ever being healed.
4. Fear of the consequences of healing.
5. Demanding that they be healed in the particular way they want, especially in physical healing.
6. Feeling that their illness is a punishment which they deserve for their sins.
7. Jealousy at other people's healings.
8. Resentment against God or others.

I always pray for faith in the "unbeliever" so that in some way they can reach out towards God's loving, healing hand. This is often a painstaking, sensitive, even thankless task, but God's love can pierce through the layers of years of wrong thinking and religious belief. In the final analysis, I believe *faith in the person to be healed merely disposes him to healing, opening his person to God's love* which then enters to heal the sick person in the best possible way. *No human being, however full of faith, can determine how God will heal him.*

Even Jesus, when he prayed in the Garden of Gethsemane, left the final result to God: "Father," he said, "if you are willing, take this cup away from me, nevertheless, let your will be done, not mine" (Luke 22: 42-43). Here is the perfect prayer of faith. Jesus prays that he would not have to suffer, but he does not know God's full will for him at this moment in the plan of salvation, so he entrusts himself to God, his Father, whom he believes can deliver him from physical suffering, but he leaves it to him. In the end, he receives great inner peace, which helps him through all the pain of his passion and death. Despite his unique prayer of faith, "God did not spare his own

Son" (Romans 8:31). From this model of prayer we can say that for those of us who want to be healed *our prayer of faith must be made*:

1. To God the Father who wants what is best for us.
2. Because God loves us as his children, and he will normally or usually heal us.
3. In trust, leaving the result to him, because no one knows God's mind fully.
4. Knowing some healing takes place, because no prayer is ever left unanswered.
5. For an increase of faith and understanding of God's will.
6. For the removal of all obstacles to God's healing power and love.
7. Believing that healing is an on-going process which makes us more aware of God's love, and our own injured person.
8. In thanksgiving for what we have received.

The Faith of the Minister of Healing

Healing has always had for me a community dimension because all Christians should believe that God is a loving Father who wants and is able to heal them. This faith has a healing effect not only on the person himself but on those around him. *A loving community of believers, trusting in God's healing love, is a most powerful healing force.* They build up each other's faith and expectancy, and that is why my ministry is always exercised in a praying and prayerful community, the centre of which is worship. In such a community there is no absolute need for any minister to move among them, or lay hands on them, because God himself is present, healing them in a far more beautiful way than could be achieved by any human instrument. Where prayer is absent or fearful, then the healing diminishes in proportion, mainly because the people are not being open to God, or to the others in the group.

One of the most beautiful services I ever attended was in Hitchin, where the mother of a severely handicapped child prayed that another severely handicapped child in the group would be healed first, before her son, "His mother needs him more," she said, "and I pray for them every day." She then laid her hands on the other boy, and got her crippled two-year-old son to do the same. On another occasion, a young man who was very immobile because of his multiple sclerosis laid hands on another man suffering from similar disease, which he so bitterly resented that it was affecting his prayer life and marriage. The healing in them and their community was tangible. The best form of healing that I have experienced is within a community where they are all praying for others, not for themselves, and where they are sensitive to the needs of the rest and are prepared to lay hands on each other when they discern that it is right to do so.

I rarely minister on a one-to-one basis, simply because God has not called me to such a ministry, whereas he obviously has done so to others. My ministry is within a group, with helpers physically, sensitively and spiritually near me who have prayed over me for some time immediately preceding the healing session. No one should minister to others unless he himself has been prayed over, been saturated in prayer himself, and asked God for discernment, guidance, wisdom and knowledge for this particular community and its unique needs, to which he is called to minister. I have heard parrot-like prayers being said over a minister of healing, and knew in my spirit that it was an "act" being gone through, rather than a time of humble preparation for the Spirit's anointing. The minister who does not constantly and genuinely ask for healing for himself is like a doctor who thinks that he is immune from the diseases he attempts to cure in others.

Ralph had a very powerful ministry of healing, but gradually more and more he ascribed the healing powers to himself, until eventually they disappeared altogether. I have also been present where, when we were supposed to be praying in the Spirit for an outpouring of his gifts, some of the group were impatient to get on with the "organization" of the healing session. Their eyes were closed in prayer, but so were their minds and hearts to what the Spirit was saying was necessary for this particular, unique session. It was a recipe for disaster with which I could not share. The group that is not sensitive to the special gifts and ministries of individuals in the group, or the uniqueness of each healing session, is closed in on itself like a spider's web. There will be a sameness and repetition in their healing sessions and approach which markedly lack the freshness of the Holy Spirit.

The power for healing remains within the praying Christian community, and great emphasis should always be placed on this community aspect of healing, however personal the healings may be. *In a sense, therefore, all Christians are healers, but they are not all healers in the same way.* "There is a variety of gifts but always the same Spirit; there are all sorts of service to be done, but always to the same Lord; working in all sorts of different ways in different people, it is the same God who is working in all of them. The particular way in which the Spirit is given to each person is for a good purpose. . . . One may have the gift of faith given by the same Spirit; another again the gift of healing, through this one spirit" (1 Corinthians 12:4-7,9). Some people within the Christian community are given gifts and ministries for the sake of the community and the mission. Such is the ministry of healing. Those chosen for this ministry receive the gift through no merit of

135

their own but through the generosity of the Spirit just as he chooses (1 Corinthians 12:11).

Every Christian group should encourage and foster the gifts and ministries of individuals, but unfortunately jealousy often enters in through some self-righteous or organizational pretext, and for the seemingly "best" of motives the community dampens, or even tries to extinguish, the flame of the Spirit. Ultimately it is the community who will suffer.

The Spirit gives to individual members not only the gift of healing, but all the other gifts which are necessary for its ministry. These are the *gifts of faith, discernment,* and the *word of knowledge. The gift of faith* means that when we minister we can pray with complete confidence that God is working and speaking through us. This is not an arrogant claim. There are those in Christian communities who, because of a false notion of humility, see this gift of faith as putting one person above the others even in a healing community, whereas they believe that all should be equal or "the same". They do not understand the nature of the gifts of the Holy Spirit, and therefore see the community in the restrictive sense of their own group, rather than in terms of the Kingdom. Abraham is our father in faith, and the Spirit raises up other Abrahams in our time if only we are humble enough to acknowledge their God-given gifts as being necessary for the spread of the Kingdom of God in our midst. The ministry is for the spread of the Kingdom. To exercise the gift of faith in a Christian community often requires fortitude as well as humility.

Ministers of healing are just the open drain pipes which the Lord uses to pour through them his healing grace to others. They believe in such a way that there is no doubt in the intention for which they are praying. This does not mean that they can predict exactly what will happen, but through this special gift they are given a more intense and a clearer insight into God the Father's dealings in healing love with the people, or person, whom he has called them to minister to at this particular moment. The more this gift of faith is exercised the more it will grow, and the humbler the ministers of healing will become. They will step out in faith in the healing ministry, but never beyond it. This is why the personal prayer life of those who minister in healing, and the prayers of others for them, is so necessary and supportive. It is a sensitive and powerful gift which is very open to abuse.

There is a danger that otherwise well-intentioned Christians will see a minister of healing at work, and try to imitate his style without having any of his gifts of faith, discernment or knowledge. These pseudo-healers do untold damage, and leave me very restless. I always check them even though they may feel rebuffed and rejected. Their hurt feelings are much the lesser of two evils. I advise (I do not say "train") groups of people at our monthly meetings, who work closely with me in the healing ministry so that at least they can avoid the more obvious pitfalls and hindrances, and at best be moved towards the actual healing ministry itself. I have seen some bizarre cases of people getting "dressed up" for the healing ministry, with large crucifixes, etc., as if they were going to a fancy dress ball. They are not suited to the gentle, peaceful, prayerful healing sessions at which I minister, or to any healing service for that matter, except to be healed themselves.

The minister of healing always needs *the gift of discernment* which helps him to discern what is the real cause, or causes, of the disease of the person before him. The human person is such a very complicated, sensitive unit, that we need the extra special guidance and diagnosis of the Holy Spirit. The "minister of healing" who has not got the gift of discernment when dealing with a particular person is just not a true minister of healing. Unfortunately, there are far too many Christians prepared to lay hands on people and who feel that this gives them the right to mumble words of diagnosis which have no relationship whatsoever to what the person needs in order to be healed. *To speak in healing without being empowered by the Holy Spirit is very wrong.* Healing is something we should enter into with great caution, and after much prayer.

The discernment of the Holy Spirit will show us what the person needs. It is not generally what he asks for, and that is why in my healing sessions I rarely ask the person before me what they want from the Lord. I find this "telling me of their ailments" a distraction, so I just ask them to pray for God's will to be done so that their real need will be discerned and healed. In this way the prayerful atmosphere of being open to God is maintained, and the gift of discernment can be used more powerfully and without hindrance.

The people who brought the paralytic to Jesus wanted him physically healed, but Jesus discerned that his real need was to have his sins forgiven. At a healing session in Birmingham, Trevor insisted on asking me to minister to him for an ulcer. I invited him to pray quietly, but he kept on insisting on telling me the full details of his abdominal trouble. Eventually, he prayed gently, and I discerned that he was suffering from an abdominal growth for whose healing I was led to pray, and by the "word of knowledge" I told him that he had just been healed of this growth. He looked at me in disbelief. "You've got it all wrong," he said "my doctor told me six months ago that I had an ulcer and I have been having special treatment for it ever since." He went away not putting a very high value on the healing ministry, and promised that this, being his first visit, would also be his last. The following week he went to the doctor, and rather mockingly told him of what had happened at the healing session, and what I had said. The doctor then replied, "Trevor, you have not got an ulcer. You never had one. We were treating you for the wrong complaint. We suspect that you may have a growth, so we are going to take some tests and a scan." These showed that Trevor had a cancerous growth which was recently healed. He came to one of our meetings later, and told us this story. Trevor, incidentally, had little or no faith when he came to his first healing session, but today he and his family have returned to the practice of their Christian faith, and his whole life, spiritual and secular, has changed.

Discernment is a gift for which all who want to be ministers of healing should pray. I have seen groups praying for inner peace for someone when they should have recognized that it was deliverance which was needed. The reverse too has often happened, and people become so obsessed with deliverance that every form of spiritual or physical pain is attributed to the machinations of the Devil. If we pray deeply, and remain open to the Spirit, then he will show us what is needed, and when to speak or remain silent. My motto in all this is quite simple "*if in any doubt whatsoever, do nothing except say a prayer for healing for the person you want to help*, and a prayer that the Holy Spirit will give to someone else at some future healing session, the true spirit of discernment and healing for this person." God alone knows when and where he is going to heal, and we are only his ministers. We need him. He does not need us. There is an arrogance in some healing groups which makes them try to heal everyone, and if they fail then they blame it all on the people on whom they have exercised their "gifts", as being lacking in faith.

The Word of Knowledge too is of invaluable assistance in healing. Through it the Spirit not only shows us that it is right to heal this person in this particular way and time, but also inspires or enlightens us to say or do something which produces a healing effect in the person for whom the message is given. This word can come in many different ways, but I have more than a strong feeling that it comes less often than I have heard many ministers of healing use it. The effectiveness and power of the "word of knowledge" is thus diminished. I use it sparingly, and if any of our group tend to use it more often, we question them and pray about it. If it is a genuine word then the Spirit will show us. I am very suspicious of some professional healers, who in large gatherings claim through the "word of knowledge" that certain people in the audience or congregation have been healed of some physical problem. If this proclamation is accompanied by "ballyhoo", then I would have to leave such a gathering as being unworthy of the beautiful, gentle ministry of healing such as I have experienced so deeply over the years in our community.

The "word of knowledge" heals. A few years ago in Manchester, at the end of a very long healing session when I was feeling quite tired, an elderly lady came forward for healing. I prayed in silence over her, and could feel a deep sorrow within her spirit. Time and again the word "flowers" came to me. I said no vocal prayer for her healing, but as she was about to go away I said, "You may think it strange, but the word I have to give you is 'flowers'." She said nothing, but turned away in her sorrow, and left the hall. A few days later she rang me up to say that she bitterly resented her husband's death, and for eight years she grieved ceaselessly. Life had come to a standstill. She came to the healing session that day as a last resort, and when I said "flowers", she knew she had never visited or tended her husband's grave. She went to a florist's immediately on leaving the hall, and visited the cemetery where she prayed at her husband's grave, and was immediately healed. It was the eighth anniversary of her husband's death.

In many other ways the Holy Spirit gives us "words of knowledge". It has played a large part in my ministry, and that is why in every healing session I move among the people in the hall or church to pray over whomsoever the Spirit leads me. I do not like people putting their hands up, or telling me what they want. Healing by the word of knowledge is very much how the Spirit moves me, but he is so unique and powerful that no one should ever lay down a hard and fast law on the minutiae of healing procedure. Healing procedures are as unique as the individuals who are healed, or who exercise the ministry of healing.

In the final analysis it is God who heals because he is a loving Father who wants us to be whole and happy. If we have faith then it is so much easier for his power to break through and transform us, but ultimately it is God alone who heals. We must never claim as ministers of healing more than the Spirit reveals to us because, in a way which we will never understand, God our loving Father is healing before our eyes if we only had the faith to see it.

11.

His Healing Touch

Jesus, the only Son of God, took flesh, "The Word was made flesh, he lived among us" (John 1:14). *In that human flesh he touched people and they were healed*. This was his *normal* way of healing, and we only have a few recorded instances of his healing at a distance. He knew the value of human contact through touch. "A leper came to him and pleaded on his knees: 'If you want to,' he said, 'you can cure me.' Feeling sorry for him, Jesus *stretched out his hand and touched him*. 'Of course, I want to,' he said. 'Be cured' and the leprosy left him at once and he was cured" (Mark 1:40-42). No one touched lepers, not only because of the risk of contagion, but also because of the Law. Jesus could have healed the leper at a distance, as he did the centurion's servant, but he "*stretched* out his hand and *touched* him" because he knew that beside the physical healing of leprosy, the leper needed to feel the loving contact of Jesus' flesh on his own. Jesus was not sanitized against human contact. Time and again in the gospel account of healing he used touch as having a special healing power of its own, and nowhere is this better illustrated than in the cure of the blind man at Bethsaida. "They came to Bethsaida, and some people brought to him a blind man whom they begged him to *touch*. He took the blind man *by the hand*, and led him outside the village. Then *putting spittle* on his eyes and *laying his hands on him*, he asked, 'Can you see anything?' The man who was beginning to see, replied 'I can see people; they look like trees to me but they are walking about.' Then *he laid his hands* on the man's eyes again and he saw clearly; he was cured, and he could see everything plainly and distinctly" (Mark 7:22-25). The whole episode centres round the healing power of touch. *Jesus held his hand* as he guided him through the village, and in their mutual physical contact the blind man felt the love of God in a human hand, and Jesus felt the human need of a blind man who longed to be healed of his affliction. Mercy and human need met, and mercy was not satisfied until the blind man "could see everything plainly and distinctly". As well as being cured of his blindness, the person and his whole being were filled with God's love through human contact.

Touch heals even without words. If you want to appreciate how highly Jesus valued the healing power of touch, then read the gospels of Matthew, Mark and Luke. The use of touch as a healing power is everywhere to be found in them. By touch there is close contact between the healer and the one to be healed. Eleanor explains the healing of touch:

> For years I had asked people to pray for me that I would find inner peace. I had countless Masses said for that intention, but somehow or other I felt the prayers that were being said for me were being said "out there", and I did not feel them in my person. I was not involved in my own healing. The prayers by someone else were doing it for me. I was not ever really healed, and never found deep inner peace of the kind I yearned for. Then one day I came to a healing session, and took part in the prayers of thanksgiving and praise before the actual healing through the laying-on of hands commenced. I felt part of a group, and when you touched someone on the head I prayed for them and their healing. When you came to me and laid your hands on me, I experienced for the first time a type of expectancy which is hard to

describe. My faith was being called on, and I responded in a personal way. Through touch I was helping myself to be healed, much as the leper in the gospel story. Within my being I called out for inner peace just as if through touch Jesus was standing over me. I was no longer one of a crowd praying for someone else. They were praying for me. I was being prayed over not only by the group but by Christ himself. It is hard to explain how I felt deep down inside me, but from that moment onwards I knew I had met Christ as a person, and had experienced an inner peace as never before. It has stayed with me these last few years, and I knew Christ had touched me and healed me the moment hands were laid on my head:

People surrounding Jesus were conscious of the healing power of touch, too. "Everyone in the crowd was trying to *touch* him because power came out of him that cured them all" (Luke 6:19). There is, of course, the famous story of the woman with the issue of blood who believed that if she could only touch the hem of his garment she would be healed (Mark 5:25-34). She decided to do so because she was afraid that because of the Law she might be considered unclean, and therefore Jesus would not touch her. This touch, even of Jesus' clothes, healed people. "The local people took all that were sick to him, begging him just to let them touch the fringe of his cloak. And all those who touched it were completely cured" (Matthew 14:35-36). John tells us in his First Letter that his subject is the Word who is life, whom "we have touched with our hands" (1 John 1:1). *Touching of, as well as by,* Jesus was equally important for healing. Ministers of healing are, in my opinion, just the garment of Jesus. If the person of Christ is not inside the garment, then what happens is deception and impersonation. People needed to be near Jesus to touch his garment, and unlike many ministers who heal from a distance by their talk or prayers, I almost always move among the crowd to be as near to them as possible. I do this not because there is anything special about me, but because there is something special in the people and it satisfies their need to be near enough to "touch the fringe of his cloak".

Joyce from Bristol explains it beautifully:

> I sat in my seat and prayed for you as you went round the church. You laid hands on some people and not on others, and I knew that God was leading you. I knew it was Christ and not you who was healing. As you passed by our bench, in my mind and heart I reached out to touch you spiritually, and I experienced a power within me just as if Christ himself had touched me. In actual fact it was Christ to whom I was reaching out.

Joyce pinpointed the healing value of touch. It calls out something within the person to be healed, whether it be faith or expectance. I place great emphasis on physical nearness, and when the Spirit moves me I always lay hands on people. It is a powerful means of bringing Christ and the person into personal contact with each other. In this way the healing becomes a person-to-person encounter. The significance and effectiveness of it cannot be overestimated.

This awareness of the sensitive, healing power of touch is to be found in the practice of the Early Church. When Peter had healed the lame man by the Beautiful Gate, he "took him *by the hand* and helped him to stand up" (Acts 3:7). "So many signs and wonders were worked among the people at the hands of the apostles that the sick were even taken out into the streets and laid on beds and sleeping-mats in the hope that at least the *shadow of Peter might fall across* some of them as he went past" (Acts 5:14-15). This healing through touch was promised by the risen Jesus: "These are the signs that will be associated with believers: they will *lay their hands on the sick* who will recover" (Mark 16:17-18). We should expect the same flow of power to pass through the apostles and disciples. Christ through us makes personal contact, physically and spiritually, with his brothers and sisters in our world, who are as desperately in need and crying out for healing as in the time of Jesus and the Early Church. If we fail to make *contact* with them, then we are in practice denying the incarnational "fleshing out" nature of Jesus' Church, and substituting in its place a ritualistic, institutional, impersonal system of healing. In no way am I attempting to devalue the Sacraments as means of healing and reconciliation, but merely pointing out that a purely mechanistic approach alone is alien to the Gospel and life-style of Jesus Christ. If we used more personal signs of healing, love and reconciliation in the Christian community, in addition to the Sacraments, then far from being devalued the Sacraments would take on a deeper meaning and become more effectively a source of renewal for the individual and for the Church.

When we relegate contact with people to the periphery of all the means God our Father wants us to use in order to become holy, then we are in danger of de-incarnationalizing and dehumanizing the Church, and emptying the Christian community of its healing role among its members and in the world. A healing church is the one which encourages and fosters the use of physical *contact* among its followers, because it sees flesh not as something evil but as an essential part of the whole person. When two or three are gathered together in Christ's name then the Lord is there in the midst of them through their incarnational contact. If the "sign of peace" at Mass is not a healing contact then we have drained it of most, if not all, of its healing power. At the same time, I am very much against those who go "over the top" at the sign of peace and go in for a hugging session. A cold, dehumanized community is not a group with whom Jesus could feel at home, or with whom he would find it easy to exercise his healing ministry.

Apart from healing by touch there are many different ways in which Jesus healed. Each way was perfectly adapted to the particular situation confronting him, and to the unique needs of the person who needed to be healed. Jesus healed:

1) through his presence
2) at a distance
3) by touch alone
4) by prayer alone
5) by touch and prayer

In this chapter I want to concentrate on the healing power of touch alone. The Catholic Church believes in the healing power of touch because in all the Sacraments, except, strangely enough, the Sacrament of reconciliation, touch is used in varying degrees in their administration. Even though I fully appreciate the healing value and significance of the laying-on of hands for healing, nevertheless I am not always led to do so. There are many occasions when I just sit, or kneel and pray for the person to be healed. One case of such a healing comes to my mind very clearly. Judith was a student at York University and was heavily involved in an evangelistic group. She felt that her work was done there and was confused as to where the Lord willed her to go next, and what exactly he wanted her to do. She came to me for help, and I invited one of our group to pray with us. We sat down quietly in chairs in different parts of the room, and it was obvious that God did not want us to lay hands on her as he was healing her directly himself. After about a quarter of an hour tears of joy flowed down her cheeks. She had received her answer, and is today a very fulfilled member of a Christian community in the South of England.

Hands should only be laid on someone when we clearly discern that it is right to do so. This should only be done after prayer, and under the guidance of the Holy Spirit. I have never experienced any presence of God or his healing power where people automatically lay their hands on my head or shoulders. They seem to go through a ritual devoid of power and meaning. The touch that heals is God's alone. He uses our hands merely as instruments of his healing power. In fact there have been times when hands have been laid on me in a group, and far from being aware of God's presence, I was quite oppressed by the physical force of people's hands, or their anxiety to let me know that the Spirit was working through them. Unless he was, and had called them to do so, then they had no right or power to lay hands on me. There were occasions too when I asked for healing through the laying-on of hands, and within seconds I found myself in the middle of a football scrum which either pushed me to the floor or nearly suffocated me from lack of air. Did they think that numbers matter when God wants to heal in a group, or that "resting in the Spirit" is always an absolutely certain sign of healing? There is a whole area of teaching to be done in this field of healing through touch. A simple warning. Beware of those who always want to lay hands on you!

Different ministers of healing use different methods of healing, especially in a large group or crowd. As I said, I almost invariably favour going among the people because this is generally what I am led to do, and it is an essential part of my ministry. To do this I need a great deal of prayerful support, because without it I soon go under with the pressure of pain and the need for healing around me. There are those who say you should never get tired during a healing session, and that this lack of tiredness is a sign of the presence of the power of the Holy Spirit. I invariably feel drained during a healing session, and need the spiritual and even physical support of a group whom I know are like-minded, and blessed with the gifts of the Spirit necessary for healing. So, whenever I move among people at a healing session, I always pray with two or three of our group beforehand so that we may be open to the Spirit, and discern what he wants us to do. I choose them after prayer, and only want them in the support group, because invariably someone wants to join our little group who inadvertently or otherwise drains us of the power of the Holy Spirit. Generally, we lay hands on each other's heads, and as a rule pray for guidance, but more often than not we kneel in silence.

In the actual healing of the larger groups, I may be moved to touch a few, or perhaps none at all, depending on the guidance of the Spirit. In no way do I have a big group with me praying for discernment, support and healing. When there are large numbers present for healing, I ask two people to stay with the person whom I have touched, or even without touch, whom I discern to be in need of further healing. In this way the healing flows through the whole group as little healing groups emerge. I am not in favour of prolonged hugging or over-concentration for a long period on one person. This is not the healing touch. If they need further healing there will be other times and places for it. There must be no confusion between the healing touch of God and merely human affection. I have found that too many people around me, far from being a support, are a distraction and even a hindrance in the healing by touch ministry, because they intrude their own needs and desires to such a degree that the person to be healed becomes more and more conscious of their presence and less and less of God's. In healing, only one person prays out loudly at any one time. The healing touch is *always gentle*. When we touch people we should have within us the mind of Christ as he moved among the sick, and the power of his Spirit to accomplish his healing work and mission. The touch can be as gentle as a feather and last just a second, like the woman from London who was healed of cancer of the ovaries by a fleeting touch on the head. We will not be conscious of ourselves, or of the need to heal, but of the love of the Father, who sends us, as he sent Christ, among his sick so that they might live the full life that he intended they should. I am never surprised by even the most sensational healings, because after all "we are the temple of God, and the Spirit of God is living among us" (1 Corinthians 3:16). God uses us and our hands just as he used the hands of Jesus to heal, and to make people aware of God's love. This is the ultimate aim and end of all touch, namely, to make people conscious of their Father's love and to respond to it.

Because healing is of its nature a very sensitive area affecting deeply the whole person, it is full of pitfalls and misrepresentation. This is especially true in the ministry of healing through the laying-on of hands. I have been asked endless questions about the various sensations one is expected to experience in one's hands when in the Spirit we lay them on someone for healing. I find these questions largely irrelevant, and often misleading, because of the danger of auto-suggestion and imitation. I can recall many people who experienced "heat", "pins and needles", "laser pains" and the like whenever I mentioned these sensations which may occur in the ministry of healing by touch. Whatever is going in the Spirit, these poor misguided, sincere people seem to want it! They desperately want to be used by God, but ultimately the selection is his. No two people minister in exactly the same way, and it is wrong to lay down universal rules to be followed slavishly in the ministry of healing by touch. Healing, I repeat, is of the person and each person is unique. For me, I find the way most effective in healing by touch is through laying the tips of my fingers on the forehead or the side temples, which help me in a way which I cannot describe to discern what healing the person truly needs, or that is already taking place. There are times too when I lay the palms of my hand on the head of the person, or on the part which needs healing, as guided by the Spirit. As a rule I experience *heat* which is common to the healing touch, and this I believe comes from inside the person to be healed through his Spirit which responds to the Spirit at work within us. The tips of the fingers being such a sensitive part of physical touch, take me, at least, right into the closest possible contact with the other, so that I am learning a language of healing as delicate as any computer system.

Many people experience a "shaking of the hands" when healing, and while this is genuine in some cases and healings have taken place, nevertheless from my own experience I am highly suspicious of it, mostly because I have had such bad experiences of it. Recently in Manchester, a lady who would dearly love to be involved in the ministry of healing, held her hands in the air where they shook violently all through the teaching. It was a distraction to me and everyone else, and when I asked her why she did it she was unable to provide an adequate answer. One of a group with whom I went to Northern Ireland did exactly the same at the drop of a hat, and at least at one point in our mission was a positive hindrance to the healing ministry in such a sensitive area of hurt. The hands of a priest who laid them on my head some years ago shook so violently that I had to ask him to stop in case he would do me permanent physical injury! In each case we must ask ourselves, "Is this what Jesus would do with his hands in this particular situation?" Perhaps I need healing of my aversion to "shaking hands", and I hope I am open to it.

In every big healing session, as a rule, I ask all the people present to *hold out their hands for the blessing of the Holy Spirit*. Then I ask them alternately to lay their hands on the people on their right and left hand side for healing. Then at the end of the session I bless their hands with oil for healing a particular person, and I can testify to the wonderful healings that have taken place through this practice. Elsewhere in this book I mentioned the restoring of eyesight to her brother by a Waterford nun whose hands were blessed for that purpose. There may be people who are unable or unwilling to come to the healing session, and I usually bless the hands of those nearest and dearest to them, so that they in turn will lay their hands on the sick person. David is one of many who was healed in this way. He was too nervous and depressed to come to the meeting for inner healing, but his wife and two teenage sons healed him through the laying on of hands which were blessed for his benefit. Whenever there is something pretty "big" that needs healing then they pray and lay hands on each other. I say "big", precisely because we can so trivialize the gift of healing through touch that we use it morning, noon and night for every form of minor ailment. The prescription I would put on the healing touch ministry is – "*To be used sparingly and only when clearly advised by the Holy Spirit.*"

As in the case of David's family, I usually bless the family as a unit, and I know of whole families who have been healed, and have returned to the practice of their faith and family prayers. In a healing session in Waterford I was moved to pray over the mother of a young family. She describes what happened.

As soon as I felt the hands on my head it was as if my whole life was being renewed, my baptism, my marriage, my family, and I knew then that I was a new person. Since that day my husband and I and our four children never miss our morning and evening prayers. Our whole family life is transformed and there is so much real love and openness between us that we have become a source of real joy to each other.

Moira and her family use the ministry of healing whenever they believe it is necessary, and it has become a source of increasing grace for inner peace in their lives.

Healing by touch should be much more common than is the practice in most Christian congregations and families today. If we confine healing to well-known ministers or lay people, and their occasional big meetings, then we have missed out on the glorious opportunity and privilege we have as ordinary Christians. All prayer groups should have regular healing sessions through the laying-on of hands as the Spirit moves them to do so. If a mother kisses her child's sore leg better, then why not lay hands on the child for wholeness and healing in a much wider and more beautiful way? The Jews have it right when they ask their father for a blessing. If the healing work, often begun at large meetings, is to continue then *the healing touch must be brought into the family as part of our normal family prayer*. Again, however, I stress the danger of trivialization, or the "magic power" of touch.

In the ministry of healing it is difficult to exaggerate the importance and effect of touch. Doctors today are being advised to pay less attention to pills and filing systems, and to give more time to the immensely more therapeutic value of touch. The taking of a person's pulse, the sounding of the lungs, and all the old-fashioned physical contacts between doctor and patient are being brought back into the forefront of medical practice today. In many cases the axiom is true, "no contact, no healing". If modern medicine leaves anything to be desired then it is in the field of personal contact and relationships, through not seeing the patient as a unique person for whom the doctor has a special care and concern.

We Christians are more at fault. True, we need healing ourselves but that should not deter us. "We are only the earthenware vessels that hold this treasure, to make it clear that such an overwhelming gift comes from God and not from us" (2 Corinthians 4:7). We are our brothers' keepers and healers. Even the way we shake hands with one another can be a wonderful healing if it is done in the name of Christ by the power of his Spirit to show God the Father's love. In order to depict creation, Michelangelo has the Father reaching out from his world to touch the tip of man's finger, and give him life. It is through us that Christ reaches out to touch and heal a wounded world. We must not be afraid to touch and heal in his name. The words of Scripture will again come true in a most wonderful way, "they will lay their hands on the sick who will recover" (Mark 16:18). It should not surprise us that when we lay hands on people they are healed. It does not mean that we are holy, but rather that as *ordinary* Christians we believe in healing, and that God our Father is prepared to use us as the garments of his Son filled with the power of the Holy Spirit. He uses the simple gift of touch, and ordinary Christians like you and me, to heal our wounded brothers and sisters so that they may live a more human, fuller, Christian life.

12.

Suffering as a Form of Healing

We all suffer and we all need healing. Yet as we look around us in the world today we are more conscious of the vast sea of suffering rather than the small islands of healing. Suffering is a mystery to the Christian, a stumbling block for the unbeliever. From the moment of pain at childbirth until our death, suffering is never far from our human experience. If God could put an end to suffering then why doesn't he? If he truly is a loving Father who has special care for us all as the pinnacle of his creation, why does it happen? What intrinsic, unique value has suffering in itself which develops and perfects us as persons, which could not be achieved by some other less painful, less seemingly destructive process? There are a myriad other questions on suffering which come to mind, and which have presented obstacles to Christian belief ever since God's only Son died a painful, shameful death on a cross. I am not even going to attempt to answer the problem of suffering for the unbeliever, and shall confine myself in this chapter to showing how suffering and healing are not mutually exclusive for the Christian. Properly understood they so complement the Gospel of Jesus Christ that to exclude or diminish the importance of one or the other is to destroy or dilute the full Gospel of a leader for whom healing was a way of life and mission, and yet who also preached that "if anyone wants to be a follower of mine let him renounce himself and take up his cross every day and follow me" (Luke 9:23).

In the life and person of Jesus the paradox of healing and

suffering finds its clearest expression. No one reading any of the four gospels can doubt the pre-eminence of Jesus as a healer. "That evening after sunset they brought to him all who were sick and those who were possessed by devils" (Mark 1:32), "and he cured them all" (Matthew 16:16). He was an enemy of all those illnesses of whatever kind which kept anyone back from loving God his Father, or from living the full human life. He showed in the clearest possible way, especially through healing, his mission of doing his Father's will. He healed, as I said before, because this is what his Father wanted him to do. The leper, for instance, was healed by Jesus (Matthew 8:3) because the Father did not want him to suffer from leprosy. His healing by Jesus was not a dispensation from the general rule of man irreversibly and intrinsically diseased, but rather a lifting of the veil of leprosy to show how man should live. Jesus, the healer of lepers, the perfect man, "like us in all things but sin", did not suffer from leprosy, or any physical or emotional disorder. These disorders or diseases were the effects of sin, which he came to heal so that he could restore man to his full health which his loving Father intended for us before sin. *If we accept the victory of Jesus over sin and death then we can no longer look on any form of human disease as inevitable or necessary.* Everything in our lives is designed to help us to grow as persons. Jesus, by his healing, showed God's plan for man not only in his own lifetime but in ours as well. Healing is essential to the Christian Gospel, and to be of value suffering must have a purpose. In no gospel account of illness do we find Jesus saying either that it was a good thing in itself, or that, even though evil, it was always good for our spiritual growth and salvation. He healed in obedience to his Father's will, and he saw healing as the ordinary and expected thing for him to do during his mission on earth.

In suffering, as in healing, he was also obedient to his

Father's will "even to accepting death, death on a cross" (Philippians 2:8). He did not want to suffer and die on a cross, nor did he completely understand its significance for himself and the world, and so he prayed, "Father, if you are willing, take this cup away from me. Nevertheless, let your will be done not mine" (Luke 22:42). The faith of Jesus, which worked so many healings among the thousands of people, now seemed to fail him when he prayed for himself. On the cross "The leaders jeered at him. 'He saved others', they said, 'let him save himself if he is the Christ of God, the chosen One'" (Luke 23:35). Jesus, in the midst of all the pain and shame of the cross, did not see his sufferings as coming from other than a loving Father who loves us, and wants us healed in a wounded, alienated world. Because his death, like his healings, was undertaken in obedience to his Father's will, so as in healing there is a hidden value in suffering, whose mystery we attempt to resolve, however minutely, in our own lives and experiences.

Jesus never looked upon suffering as a punishment sent by a vengeful God who gloried in pain. For him, suffering had a positive, creative, spiritual meaning. After his resurrection, he reminded his apostles that he had foretold what would happen to him. "He opened their minds to understand the scriptures and said to them, 'This is what is written: the Messiah must suffer and must rise from death three days later and in his name forgiveness of sins must be preached to all nations'" (Luke 24:46-47). When Peter, as leader of the apostles, had reacted strongly against Jesus' prophecy that he would suffer grievously at the hands of the chief priests, elders and scribes (Matthew 16:22), Jesus rounded on him, "Get behind me, Satan: You are an obstacle in my path because the way you think is not God's way but man's" (Matthew 16:23). As I said in an earlier chapter, Jesus showed by his death, in the clearest possible way, our love through him for the Father, and his love for us. *It is only when we begin to understand healing that our perception of the mystery of suffering will grow and vice versa.* An exaggeration of one or the other destroys the balance of the Gospel, and of Jesus' life and example. It is really only since I myself became heavily involved in the healing ministry that I have really begun to grow in my true and honest appreciation of the part that suffering plays in my own spiritual life, and those of my Christian brothers and sisters.

The difficulty we have today in accepting and understanding healing would not have arisen for the Early Church Christians. They looked at health and healing as the ordinary response of God their Father, whose love wanted to heal them. Healing was one of the most important ministries of a young Church eager to evangelize and spread the Gospel of Jesus Christ. Later on the pendulum swung away dramatically and almost exclusively to highlighting the spiritual importance, even necessity, of suffering in all its many forms. Those who suffered most, irrespective of the nature of their sufferings, or their attitude to it, were told that "those whom God loves most suffer most". Suffering in itself became a sign almost of predestination, and immediate entry into heaven, because the sick did their purgatory on earth. Suffering came to be looked on as such a blessing from God that it was wrong to pray for healing. Many saints of centuries past prayed for more pain and more grace, but never for healing. Healing, they thought, would deprive them of the more perfect imitation of Christ and divert them from the path to heroic sanctity. Today the pendulum has swung so sharply in reaction to this exclusive emphasis on the healing, redemptive value of suffering, that for some, all suffering is regarded as an absolute evil and is due to the personal sin or lack of faith in the diseased person. They claim that suffering, whether physical, moral, emotional or spiritual, can always be eradicated from a true Christian's life. The actual healing, whose source is God's love and power, is up to the individual. He is told without much further explanation, "Your healing is within you". In this philosophy, "healing is in, suffering is out". I do not ascribe to either of these exclusive attitudes of complete healing or blind suffering, because they are alien to the full Gospel of Christ to which both suffering and healing are indispensable and complementary. *I believe that any suffering, of whatever kind, which prevents us from living a fully human Christian life can and should be healed.* God our Father does not want us to suffer pointlessly, or to imagine that suffering in itself pleases him. There are millions of people today who suffer needlessly and aimlessly because we in the Church have not preached the Gospel of healing or brought its light to bear on human suffering. Too many people are broken in a *destructive* way, which gives glory neither to God nor to man. They blame God for their suffering and hate him for it, thus adding to their inner turmoil because they have been taught that suffering is a good thing sent by a loving God.

I have met hundreds of bitter people like Robert, who come endlessly to every healing session they can, yet who invariably end up in deeper despair than before. Robert, through no fault of his own, developed a deep hatred of his mother, who from his earliest years had so projected her dependence on him that he was unable to break away from her. He could not form any meaningful relationships with anyone else, especially those of the opposite sex. "I hate my mother today", he told me, "more than ever before. I am a homosexual, and because she taught me that this was a perverted condition, I hate myself. I am now in my late forties, terribly lonely, shall never marry, and am caught up in a religion whose rules I detest. As for God, I just hate him with every fibre of my twisted being. I didn't ask to be born or to have the possessive mother I have, so why did he do this to me? Some day I shall take my own life, and that is the only way I can get even with them all."

There is no point in telling Robert to "grin and bear it", or as Christ said to Saint Paul, "My grace is enough for you: my power is at its best in weakness" (2 Corinthians 12:9). I have heard such spiritual maxims being peddled unthinkingly, and with disastrous effects, to tortured people like Robert. What he needs, and I have worked on it with him with little apparent success so far, is the healing of memories so that he can come to terms with his mother and learn to forgive her. He must also come to terms with God, and look on him as a loving Father. This he is now beginning to do through identification with the suffering Christ whom he loves. If his hero "Christ" could accept suffering from a loving Father, then why shouldn't he? Always I have found that this hatred of God the Father is best approached and healed through love of the suffering Christ, and identifying acceptance with him of his own suffering. When and if this is done, we can then together pray through the general mould of his life, and discern what God as a loving Father wants him to do. Will he remain homosexual and, if so, how positively fulfilling can his life become? I do not know the answer yet. One thing I am *certain* of is that God never intended Robert to live unhealed like this, and that it is our Christian obligation in service to the Gospel to set him free.

All suffering must be examined in the light of the Gospel, and in obedience to Christ's command to heal the brethren. The Spirit will send his gifts of faith, discernment and knowledge upon us so that when healing comes, any suffering which may remain will be creative, purposeful and be united to Christ's *loving* surrender of himself to his Father. We must always keep before our minds the belief that God our loving Father wants the person to be healed infinitely more than we do. *It is the whole person whom God the Father wants healing, and not necessarily the part which seems more obvious to our human veiled eyes.* James was blind from birth, and his friends brought him to one of our healing sessions, ostensibly for the miracle of sight. After silent prayer over him, I received the discernment of his need for inner peace. I prayed for this while gently laying my hands on his head, not on his eyes. He told me afterwards,

> For years I have been to healing sessions and every time, the people who want to heal me touch my eyes and ask for the gift of sight for me. What I have really craved for all these years was inner peace of mind and soul, but no one prayed for it. I have been tortured for years, not by my lack of sight, but my lack of the presence of God, and of his peace. When I felt the touch of your hands it was like a spiritual rebirth, and my soul was flooded with a peace I had never experienced before. I could praise God with an unfettered heart. People think I resent my blindness. They are wrong. I'm used to being blind, but I needed that inner peace so that I could be aware of myself as a whole person.

James was healed of dryness of soul, but not of his physical blindness, so in that sense he is still not a whole person, but then, as I have said repeatedly, every person needs constant healing. However, what was destroying him spiritually was not his blindness but his lack of inner peace. Both his lack of inner peace and his blindness were the result, ultimately, of sin in our world. His lack of sight is a reminder that we live in a wounded world. I only wish that those who see with eyes in our world had the gift of inner peace which is James' today. He is far more whole and healthy than they are. In a special way which worldly people will not accept or appreciate, *his blindness does not prevent him living the full, human, Christian life* intended by God his loving Father, because his total, loving acceptance of his blindness has linked him into the sufferings of Christ, and his loving obedience to his Father. In a beautiful way through the positive use he has made of his blindness, he is a much finer, more sensitive Christian person who has developed his other God-given talents. The power of Christ's resurrection broke through the spiritual death within James' soul, and I completely believe that when it is right for James to be given the gift of sight *he will see*. This restoration of sight will come if his physical blindness detracts essentially from his relationship with God, his neighbour, and within himself. If, in the future, I or somebody else were given the gift of discerning that he should see because this was necessary to his Christian life, I would have no hesitation in praying for his physical healing, or believing that it would happen. His blindness, through the effect of sin, has been overcome through the grace of Christ in so many ways that it has lost its sting for him as a person.

The important thing therefore in healing is discernment and how to deal with the individual people who come to us for healing. *We have to discern what God wants for this individual at this particular moment in his life.* The reason why people are not healed as they should be lies generally not with them, certainly not with God, but probably with us. There are "healers" who seem "to know" what people need just by looking at them, and then proceed to tell God what they want him to do. James is typical of many such cases with which I could fill this book, but another example may help to drive home the point. A prayer group in Lincoln had been praying for six months prior to my visit, for Rachel, a young woman of eighteen years who had been badly stricken by polio when she was four years old.

There was an air of expectancy at the meeting and everyone was waiting for a spectacular physical healing. In the afternoon the big moment came and we all prayed for Rachel, who looked a very sad young lady. As I prayed over Rachel my eyes were drawn to a middle-aged couple who looked uncomfortable and full of sorrow. I "knew" that they were part of the healing process and so I called them forward. No one told me that they were, in fact, Rachel's parents. As I laid hands on Rachel I discovered an inner sadness which struck down to the roots of her inner being much deeper than any polio. Gently she turned to her parents and quietly, but near to tears, she said, "I am your only child and you must be disappointed to see me like this, when you might have expected a much prettier daughter who might soon be getting married. I've prayed to get well, and I'm sorry it has not worked out that way, but what really grieves me, is that through all the years since I contracted the polio you never once told me, either that you loved me or wanted me. I'm sorry to be like this and I can cope with my disability but my loneliness is like a naked sword within me." The parents were completely reconciled with their daughter. After Rachel had contracted polio they never spoke to each other about it, and agreed to have no more children. Their home was a desert of loneliness, bitterness and recrimination. Today it is full of joy and peace. The moral of the story is *never to pray for what you see people seem to want, but in faith, leave it to God to show you what they need deep down within themselves.* We see only part of a human being but God sees in total. He knows the whole person.

In attempting a deeper understanding of suffering and healing, it is absolutely necessary that we *prepare properly for every healing session*, with *minds open to God's plan* for this person to be healed whom he loves and wants to make whole. Wholeness *in this life* does not mean an end to all forms of illness, whether physical, emotional or spiritual, and it certainly does not mean an end to death. The Spirit will guide our minds and hearts and show us what to pray for and how. The story of the epileptic demoniac highlights how thorough our preparation must be when we pray for healing. "When they [Jesus, with Peter, James and John] rejoined the rest of the disciples, they saw a large crowd round them and some teachers of the law arguing with them. When the people saw Jesus, they were greatly surprised and ran to him and greeted him. Jesus asked his disciples, 'what are you arguing with them about?' A man in the crowd answered, 'Teacher, I brought my son to you because he has an evil spirit in him and cannot talk. Whenever the spirit attacks him, it throws him to the ground and he foams at the mouth, grits his teeth, and becomes stiff all over. I asked your disciples to drive the spirit out, but they could not.' Jesus said to them, 'How unbelieving you people are: How long must I stay with you? Bring the boy to me!' They brought the boy to Jesus. As soon as the spirit saw Jesus, it threw the boy into a fit, so that he fell on the ground and rolled round, foaming at the mouth. 'How long has he been like this?' Jesus asked the father. 'Ever since he was a child', he replied. 'Many times the spirit has tried to kill him by throwing him in the fire and into water. Have pity on us and help us, if you possibly can!' 'Yes', said Jesus, 'if you yourself can. Everything is possible for the person who has faith.' The father at once cried out, 'I do have faith, but not enough. Help me to have more.' Jesus noticed that the crowd was closing in on them, so he gave a command to the evil spirit. 'Deaf and dumb spirit,' he said, 'I order you to come out of the boy and never go into him again!' The spirit screamed, threw the boy into a bad fit and came out. The boy looked like a dead corpse and everyone said, 'He is dead'. But Jesus took the boy by the hand and helped him to rise, and he stood up. After Jesus had gone indoors, his disciples asked him privately, 'Why couldn't we drive the spirit out?' 'Only prayer and fasting can drive this kind out', he answered them. 'Nothing else can'" (Mark 9:14-29).

Notice how thorough Jesus' preparation is before he actually heals the boy. He asks questions, observes the nature of the convulsions, demands faith from the father and the bystanders — "everything is possible for anyone who has faith" (9:23) – and only then does he heal the boy. His disciples, who had performed so many healings already, had forgotten to prepare properly by prayer and fasting for this particular healing. Each healing, like each person, is unique.

As a general rule it is best not to prepare exclusively for any particular healing, as happened in Rachel's case. By all means the people in the prayer group were right to pray for Rachel's physical healing, but their prayers should not have been confined to that alone. We should pray and prepare for God's loving, healing will to be done. What could be better or more effective? Time and again I am presented with people for whose healing sufficient or open preparation has not been undertaken, as if healing is the result of a conveyor belt process with automatic and identical results. So many people come along to healing sessions and mention some physical, emotional or spiritual problem, and expect to be healed immediately, as if by some magic touch with mysterious healing power. I am totally against "instant healing" which is isolated from prayer. I believe that if the Christian community really prayed for true healing of the person rather than the "bits and pieces", then our world would witness even more the amazing power of healing.

There are thousands of people in my experience who are not healed because of the lack of discernment and faith in those who pray for them. The reasons they do not pray properly have their origins in false concepts of suffering, healing, and God's will for us as his loving Father. If people are not healed in our eyes it is because our vision is superficial, and our desire is often for the spectacular. I would like to go on record as stating that I have never known a single person in good faith, over whom our group has been led to pray, who has not received a healing from God. This is what I expect because God always answers our prayers, but often not in the way we ask. It is because we do not see *our* end result in healing that we fail to see God's healing power at work in the person he loves as his child. His ways are deeper and better than ours. Generally I pray for inner healing but this extends in many, many cases to physical healing, even of the most dramatic kind; but the healings are always of the person. This is in no way due to anything in me but to God's power alone.

He never fails the person because he loves them as the individual he created, redeemed through his Son, and sanctified through his Spirit. I am not saying I always knew what the healings were, or that they took place immediately, but I am affirming that if we all do what is required of us as a healing Christian community then healing will take place. People have got annoyed and frustrated with me whenever I have refused to pray for a particular healing, especially a physical one, when they have not prepared properly or sufficiently for it, or when I am not led by the Spirit to do so. God cannot be called on by us to show how great we are, and that we have a "hot line" to him. Rather, he calls on us to show how loving he is, and that we are only the telegraph poles which carry the message to the sick person to whom he speaks personally in healing love. God heals the individual in a person-to-person encounter; we in the healing community will always remain the open channel for their communication.

But, is the statement "God always heals when we ask properly, and if no healing takes place then we have not asked properly", an easy opt-out for God? What about the people suffering from the most horrible physical and mental disorders which so affect them that they and those around them find it hard to believe in God? Surely if God is a loving Father he would not create and leave on this earth such less-than-human persons? My answer from my own experience in the healing ministry is direct and simple. We do not understand the mystery, not only of God, but of the human person. Many people whom the world considers handicapped and abnormal are much more human, loving and truly normal than their so-called superiors. I am not glorifying suffering, but rather testifying to the mystery and deep-seated richness of the human person.

Maurice is a badly crippled boy who has been in a comatose state for many years. I "know" that within him there is a peace which is quite beautiful. Through it he has reconciled his parents to each other, and has uncovered a wealth of love among his helpers which I believe would not have been possible if he were other than he is. I am not saying his condition is the price of their peace, or even asking why he should pay it, but his *person* is full of happiness. Even though he has not spoken for years, I consider him to be a very outgoing, healing personality. He generates love not pity, and those near him experience it in a fulfilling way. His physical suffering does not in my discernment hinder him from living a fully human Christian life. He may not be able physically or intellectually to do most things that his "normal" peers are expected to do, but then they are not as mature and peaceful as he is. What does it mean to be fully human anyway?

We cannot understand healing if we do not appreciate the spiritual value and significance of suffering in relation to the whole person. If suffering had no value the healing of everyone of every illness would be the only way of supporting our belief in a loving God who is our caring Father, but *suffering has a value* and there are as many approaches to healing as there are to suffering. Those who disagree with my views on healing probably do so because they cannot accept my biblical and practical interpretation of suffering, as outlined in the chapter "Disease and Remedy". For me, suffering will always be with us and is an evil consequent on the fall of man. No one would have been born or lived with any form of disease or death if sin had not entered our world. Even though Jesus conquered "sin, death and the world", the effects of sin remain within us as persons, affecting our bodies, emotions, spirits and souls. This is why disease in all its forms is so apparent in our weakened world and human person. But the Christian has a new creative attitude to suffering because Christ has given him the victory over it.

Suffering is and should be redemptive. With St Paul we say, "I want only the perfection that comes through faith in Christ, and is from God and based on faith. All I want, is to know Christ and the power of his resurrection and to share his sufferings by reproducing the pattern of his death. That is the way I can hope to take my place in the resurrection of the dead" (Philippians 3:9-11). Suffering that is not redemptive and fulfilling of the person and his destiny is destructive. The tragedy is not that there is suffering in the world but that we waste it so foolishly. Suffering in itself, like poverty, is evil. To suffer for suffering's sake is un-Christian, and a pale imitation of the Spartans of old, as if Jesus Christ had not entered our world and shot suffering through with the light and power of his resurrection. Suffering, like poverty, has its only value in that it gives us the power-base from which to love and grow as persons. Suffering that is "cross-centred", without the resurrection, is often one of the big obstacles I encounter in the ministry of healing. *Suffering* that is linked to Christ's loving obedience to his Father and is accepted in that way *is a very important healing factor in our lives.* We must not glorify suffering in itself any more than we should glorify healing from every form of suffering in our lives. *Suffering, like healing, has to be prayed about so that we may receive a truer discernment of its meaning in our lives.*

Suffering heals:-

1. When it is positive and helps us to grow as persons.
2. When it enables us to have a deeper, fuller, loving relationship with God, our neighbour and within ourselves.
3. When, not understanding its mystery in our lives, we unite it with Jesus' suffering in the Garden of Gethsemane and become more Christ-like in our acceptance of the unknown.
4. When it increases our faith and trust in God our Father to whom we commit our lives.
5. When it grows into *compassion* for others in the Church and the world.
6. When we have prayed over it with the gift of discernment.

There are myriad biblical texts which I could quote – such as 1 Peter 4:1-3, Romans 8:18, 2 Corinthians 1:5-7 – which demonstrate that suffering remains a part, albeit constructive, of our lives as Christians. We always need healing. Suffering is linked to healing, to a greater understanding of ourselves as persons, and to our mission to spread the Kingdom of God's love on earth. As we appreciate and discern the positive side of suffering, people will be healed more and more so as to live the good life, as God our loving Father intended they should. In this way our suffering is like the cry of childbirth of the new creation come alive within ourselves and our world. "It was not through any fault on the part of creation that it was made unable to attain its purpose, it was made so by God; but creation still retains the hope of being freed, like us, from its slavery to decadence to enjoy the same freedom and glory as the children of God. From the beginning until now the entire creation, as we know, has been groaning in one great act of giving birth, and not only creation but all of us who possess the first fruits of the Spirit, we too groan inwardly as we wait for our bodies to be set free. For it was by hope that we were saved" (Romans 8:20-24).

13.

The Healing of Memories, Guilt and Fear

Christian Healing, Medicine and Psychiatry

God the Father wants to heal the whole person. As individuals we are not only what we ourselves have received from people and events in our lives, but what they have received from us. We are children of today who go back in history to the time when human beings first lived on our earth. Our "family tree" is not limited to the third and fourth generation. Powerful forces in our emotional psychological make-up, hidden from the most penetrating psychiatrists, hold us bound, so that we cannot live the full Christian life as God the Father intended we should. Jesus came to set the prisoners free, and the greatest field for Christian healing, yet still relatively unexplored, is the inner emotional structure of the human person. It deeply affects our soul and body, and is also affected by them, because the human person is a unit. For example, a person who is chronically depressed cannot always in truth and conscience praise God when his depression affects his physical body and his whole way of living. Through inner healing we can, by the power of the Holy Spirit, and by using all the medical and psychological skills available to us, set such a person free, when we discern that his disorders are destructive of his human and spiritual life. The healing of memories and the eradication of false guilt and irrational fear are three of the most important areas of inner healing.

Most doctors and psychiatrists would welcome our help in healing, even in the field of what they consider to be their special skills and expertise, because their knowledge of the complexity of the human person is understandably limited. A well-known orthopaedic consultant told me, "I can perform two hip replacements, and as far as the operations go they should both work equally well. With one person everything is well-nigh perfect, while the operation for the other person is a disaster and never works properly. I cannot explain it except in terms of different attitudes, outlooks, something in their emotional make-up which sets up the positive or negative reaction. If someone like a priest could help them to have a positive attitude to their operation, heal their minds and emotions in fact, then our medical work would be much more successful." There are some Christians who practise inner healing who would dismiss psychiatrists and doctors as irrelevant and even harmful to the care and healing of people. They claim that God alone can heal, and has no need of doctors, psychiatrists and their "artificial" medicines and remedies. I do not subscribe to that view.

It is true that God sometimes heals immediately and directly without the intervention and aid of anyone, be they doctor, psychiatrist or Christian healer. Generally, however, he works through nature and the skills of those who sincerely wish people to live a fuller, more human, meaningful life. Where these skills and aids help us in the healing of a diseased person, then we must make use of them. When the medical and psychiatric skills are saturated in healing Christian prayer, then we are showing how God uses us at all levels to help and heal each other. The Christian healer who makes exaggerated claims, especially for physical healing, which take no account of other natural skills, is leaving the Christian healing ministry open to ridicule. In the same way, doctors and psychiatrists should acknowledge that in many cases with which they deal there is a spiritual element at work which is effecting as much healing, if not far more, than they could ever hope to do.

Genevieve is one example. She had severe cancer of the liver and was told she was inoperable. We prayed over her for inner healing from fear, and also for skill for the surgeon. Her operation was *extraordinarily* successful in the judgement of the surgeon, and it was clear to all concerned that there were inner healing forces at work healing her, so that today she is well on the way to complete physical recovery. In both aspects of her healing the power of God was at work. The relationship of medicine and psychiatry to Christian healing is being keenly examined more seriously and openly, and when the three forces work together for the good of the whole person then we will all gain a deeper insight into the complexity of our human nature and personality. Doctors and psychiatrists are also healers if by their skill they help to set people free to live a fuller human life. They are complementary healers with those of us who believe and practise Christian healing.

Memories

Many people are crippled in their emotions, and a large part of their suffering comes from emotional wounds of the past, some of which lie in conscious memory, and others remain from previous generations. This latter is called the healing of the "Family Tree". In other words, we live in a damaged world in which we have been injured especially by those nearest and dearest to us. Most people push these hurts deep down into their subconscious and suppress them, or dwell on them negatively until they affect their whole lives, spiritually, emotionally and physically, so that the hurt makes them a different person to the one they should be. They think they can forget the hurt, and yet if they want to be healed, to be set free, so that they can become the whole person God the Father wants them to be, then the hurt must be brought to the surface in a positively healing way. It is not enough just to live through the hurt so that then you can say you are "healed", as some psychiatrists hold. As Christian healers we bring the hurt to light *through praying* with the person, and *in prayer* sustain him as *he brings the pain to Jesus Christ*, the wounded healer. In the power of the Spirit we ask the Father to heal him.

Often the inner healing takes more than one session, and both the person to be healed and those who minister healing, must be sensitive and patient as they wait on the Lord. The first healing is generally a very painful one, as the full realization of the injury bursts in upon the consciousness of the damaged person. It may evoke anger, bitterness or a thousand other emotional reactions, but these are to be expected and prayed through. John was very bitter about his stepfather, who made him the scapegoat of everything that went wrong in the home. Whatever happened John was blamed, and so he completely retired into his defensive shell of non-communication with everybody. When we prayed with him through his early days the hatred he felt for his stepfather came pouring out, and visibly shook many of those who were helping me to minister to him. It took three sessions before we came to the final one of release in which John was genuinely able to forgive his stepfather from his heart. His whole personality and even his body changed. His arthritis and headaches disappeared, he became a much more open, joyful and caring person, his relationship with his mother was transformed, and soon he is getting married, a state he would never have contemplated years ago because he was incapable of forming a loving relationship.

Forgiveness is of the Essence of the Healing of Memories

This requires the person to enter sympathetically into the mind and heart of the one who damaged him. So much of our emotional and physical sickness is due to our unwillingness or inability to forgive, that before praying for any healing I always begin with a prayer of forgiveness and repentance, "When you stand in prayer, forgive whatever you have against anybody, so that your Father in heaven may forgive you your failings too" (Mark 11:25). When we empty ourselves of our anger, hatred, revenge or other dark feelings, then the light of God's loving mercy flows into our lives. The lack of forgiveness which was the blockage to God's healing leaves a void caused by the hurtful memory which needs filling up. This filling up with the love and power of the Holy Spirit which transforms our lives is one of the most beautiful and enlivening forms of healing. I have witnessed it so often in Northern Ireland.

For six months I worked with a group of Peace People from Northern Ireland. They were all hurting deep inside from the tribal conflict which had torn their land and themselves apart. So many of them had suffered the death of a loved one through violence, or had been "brainwashed" into a negative sectarian way of spontaneous reaction to the other side. You could sense the bigotry and distrust beneath their otherwise sincere attempt to get to know each other. They needed more than human dialogue. We began to pray deeply for the hurts inside each one of them, and for forgiveness of those who had indoctrinated them. The healing of memories in that situation made me more aware than anything else of the mountain of inner healing that is needed in Northern Ireland. Mary from East Belfast wanted to be healed of most distressing memories.

Much as I tried to forgive Catholics, something always happened to bring out all the bile and hatred. The killing of a friend's husband, the bombings, the threats of violence, drove me back into my own Protestant ghetto where I felt secure in all the bitter and vengeful remarks. I found it hard to return to the prayer group and ask forgiveness of Catholics when they were still causing the hurt. I just hadn't it in me, nothing, only black despair, and the uncontrollable urge to strike back. I suppose as long as I live here I shall always find it difficult, but strangely enough the more I forgive people who hurt me the closer I come to Christ and the suffering he endured to bring us his peace.

Mary has grown spiritually, and has received many healings this past ten years. She knows the pain of hurtful memories and was not healed once and for all, but whenever the pain bruises her again she knows where to go for release and healing.

Love is the Only Healing Remedy

This is so true for those who are bitter or resentful. I have found that many physical diseases, such as asthma or certain types of arthritis, are healed once the barriers of revenge or bitterness or the other destructive elements of our human personality are removed by love. Love melts the coldness of hurtful memories, and I have often found that when the person is being healed his body begins to radiate heat. The interplay of emotions and physical reactions is very much in evidence in healing. Often when people seek a physical healing, the source of their disorder is due to some emotional upset which in turn has a spiritual basis. A very high percentage of emotional diseases to which I have ministered in healing is caused by an awareness of being unloved in childhood, which breeds a sense of worthlessness of oneself, and resentment of one's parents. There is no need for me to give even a single case history of this type of emotional deformity. It is very much a matter of the sins and deficiencies of the parents being visited on the children. In ministering to the victims of such poor background it is essential that a sympathetic silence be observed, and that no more than two or three trusted people be present. I have been quite shocked to learn of the violation of confidences given in such an intimate and sacred setting. This does untold harm to the integrity and credibility of the whole healing ministry, and in Catholic terms I would equate it with a violation of the "seal of confession".

In the *healing of memories*, these are the important points to note:

1. It is the most frequent cause of physical, emotional and spiritual hurt.
2. Most hurt is caused in childhood or from the "family tree".
3. Forgiveness and love are the essence of inner healing.
4. Silence, patience, sympathy, the keeping of confidences, are essential for the small healing group of no more than three persons.
5. The hurt must be brought to Jesus the wounded healer.

Guilt

Just as forgiveness is essential in the healing of the hurtful memories so it is also an absolutely necessary ingredient in the eradication of false guilt. In hurtful memories the person has to *forgive others*, whereas in false guilt he has to *forgive himself*. Strange as it may seem, this forgiveness of oneself, in healing terms of sensitivity and length of time, is much more difficult than the healing of hurtful memories or any other form of inner healing. All that I have written so far in this chapter about the healing treatment recommended for those who suffer from hurtful memories is equally true in our dealings with those who suffer from false guilt and irrational fear. The chapter on "Learning to Love Yourself and Be Healed" is especially relevant to those who are plagued with false guilt feelings. Immoral attitudes and actions give rise to true guilt, which in turn generates an awareness of our failure to love and serve God, our neighbour, and ourselves as we should do. Today many negative-thinking people say that we have lost the sense of sin. I believe *we have lost the sense of forgiveness*. Until we forgive ourselves as God our loving Father does, then we will adopt a false sense of extreme values of either selfishly putting ourselves above everyone else's interests, or downgrading ourselves as not being worthy of anyone's love, least of all our own. God becomes the monster and judge, or the "unreachable Holy One – out there", whom we will never touch, or have the courage to meet in any form or dialogue.

Just as permissiveness is condemned in society, I equally reprove those people who, in the name of Christ and his Church, excessively preach "hell's fire and damnation". "Alas for you, scribes and Pharisees, you hypocrites: You who shut up the Kingdom of Heaven in men's faces, neither going in yourselves nor allowing others to go in who want to. . . . You tie up heavy burdens and lay them on men's shoulders, but will you lift a finger to move them? Not you!" (Matthew 23:13,4). The churches that constantly harp on about guilt are building up not repentance but neurosis in many of their followers. There are as many forms of false guilt as there are people who are crippled by it. *It is a form of spiritual leukaemia which drains the person of life and love.*

One of the commonest forms which false guilt takes is where *the person believes that his present spiritual, physical and emotional distress is due to some of his actions in the past, especially those related to sex*. The number of people who suffer from this destructive form of guilt is horrendously large. Joan was sexually abused by her uncle when she was six years old. She came to our healing session twenty-six years later in what I can only describe as a "terrible mess".

I have been in and out of psychiatric hospitals but I wasn't healed because I didn't want to be. I felt I deserved the punishment because of what I did. I have forgiven my uncle long ago because he was a weak man, and had had too much to drink anyway. I cannot forgive myself and I don't want to. I have never really prayed to God as someone who loves me because I know he just couldn't after what I have done. I get terrible fits of depression, and I would have committed suicide a long time ago but that would have been the easy way out. As for marriage, who would want me anyway because I am soiled, and sex is a dirty thing. I have lost contact with my family and never visit my old home because of the hurtful memories it stirs up within me.

Joan is now completely healed of her false sense of guilt, the pains and aches in her body have disappeared, and, having forgiven herself, her whole life has undergone a gradual transformation. It took four sessions before she was eventually restored to her rightful assessment of herself as a person whom God loves. Her treatment was extremely sensitive, and we had only one "hiccup", when an over-zealous person got in among our healing team and told her to "snap out of it". "Fast healing" does for our spiritual growth what "fast food" does for our digestive system! Joan did not need a psychiatrist, her chronic asthma was cleared up completely, and her relationship with her family is totally restored. God in his healing power broke the vicious circle of false guilt which was destroying her as a person and bringing her life to a standstill.

False guilt is invariably caused by *a wrong concept of God not as a Father but as a vengeful judge*. The chapters, "The Father Who Wants to Heal Us" and "Our Healing with God", may help to heal those who suffer from this form of false guilt because of some "unforgivable" sins in their past life. No amount of rational discussion will help them because, after interminably long discussions, going over the same ground repeatedly and ending in what seems like success, they are soon back on the "guilt merry-go-round" and no one can prise them off it. They need the healing which God alone can give. If anyone doubts the evils of preaching to excess the God who punishes sinners, then he should come to one of our healing sessions. Where the threat of divine sanctions is imposed on a person already prone to self-doubt and self-recrimination then the recipe for disaster is well-nigh perfect.

Probably the most difficult ones to deal with in regard to false guilt, in so far as they resist strongly any form of inner healing, are the *scrupulous*. They are a curious and tortured mixture of self-righteousness and self-condemnation. During our mission in Ireland last year we were constantly questioned by a scrupulous lady who vacillated between praising God for all the healings that were taking place, and condemning us for daring to release people from "the crosses that were the means of their salvation". A false concept of suffering, and a cross-centred spirituality without the light and hope of the resurrection, have done immeasurable damage to the natural, as well as supernatural, lives of many people. Peter was so scrupulous that physically he was nearly bent in two, and his emotional life was a living hell on earth. He talked at length to me about it.

As a child, I was very sensitive about myself and I was afraid of being laughed at. I developed a very strict code of self-discipline, too strict in fact, so that no one could point an accusing finger at me. I went to church regularly, and ended up going every day: I reached the stage where if I missed a day at church, I would feel horribly guilty about it. I was so anxious to win God's love that I subjected myself to fasts and doing without things which brought any sense of enjoyment or pleasure into my life. The voice of my conscience was always at my ear, and I obeyed all its whispered commands. I saw sin where there was no sin at all. I didn't hate or blame anyone for this. I just blame myself.

Peter is gradually being healed, but helping him is like trying to pull a mule out of a bog! The hallmark of so many scrupulous people is that they try to win God's approval by their own efforts. Peter's poor physical, mental and emotional condition is obviously due to an exaggerated response to false teaching on the nature of God and salvation. He is being healed but the wounds still lie deep.

Irrational Fear

Irrational fear, like false guilt, is a force which is most destructive of every aspect of human life. *The fearful person is a diminished person*. Envy, lack of self-confidence, dread of failure, sense of inferiority, they are all side-effects of the disease of fear. Much of what is good in our lives never sees the light of day because it remains enshrouded in the darkness of fear. One of the worst kinds of fear is that which affects our souls and spirits. We are so slavishly afraid of God that we are afraid to love him. Just as in false guilt there is a lack of forgiveness of ourselves, so in irrational fear there is a lack of faith and trust in God to provide for all our needs. So the fearful person, wanting to be in control of everything around him, often desires to become the dominant power-person. Fear spawns power, with its attendant evils which surround us everywhere, even in ecclesiastical organizations. We have to come face to face with the fears, not only around us but within ourselves, which hinder us from growing to maturity as persons. We are even afraid to be ourselves. Fear, therefore, damages our relationships with God, with others and within ourselves.

Our *Christian faith overcomes our fear* and helps us to become more fully human and alive. Jim was a perfect example of a body and soul being wasted through fear.

> I lived in a cage of fear, and I was unable to break loose. I was afraid of what people thought of me, afraid to take the initiative in anything. I agreed with people, even when I knew in my heart they were wrong, and I hated them and myself for being in such a situation. Fear is such a powerful force that it warped my judgement of myself, my family and even of God. When I came to a healing session I wanted to be healed, and yet I held back because I was afraid of the consequences, afraid I would have to change. So I did not come forward for healing. I was glad and terribly disappointed; glad that I didn't have hands laid on me, and disappointed because I still had my fear. In two further sessions I came forward for healing, and you said nothing could be done for me unless I got rid of my fear. I was angry with you at first, but you were right. I knew something had to be done, so for weeks I prayed for the faith I needed to rid me of the fear which haunted my life. Then in faith, at the next session I came forward for healing, and how wonderfully liberating it all was. To think I was living so much of my life in fear makes my blood run cold if I didn't have the warmth of knowing that now I am trying to live a full Christian life in which I believe and trust in God to provide and watch over me.

Jim was healed of many physical and emotional illnesses in that single session once he threw off the shackles of fear. As a minister of healing I have never been able to channel God's healing power to anyone who is in the grip of fear, except to pray for their release and healing from it. Fear is a locked door which has to be opened before anything else within the person can be healed. Fearful people are as cold and dead as something from a deepfreeze. Their fear sometimes becomes so oppressive that they need deliverance from it.

Fear, like faith, is very personal. Fear affects everyone born into this world darkened by the shadow of sin. Even Jesus himself knew the pain of fear of suffering and death in the Garden of Gethsemane: "My soul is sorrowful to the point of death . . . My Father, if it is possible, let this cup pass me by. Nevertheless, let it be as you, not I, would have it" (Matthew 26:38-39). Jesus' personal faith overcame his fear, and it is by personal faith that those who are harassed by fear will be healed. When we study the Gospel we see how Peter himself denied Jesus because of fear (John 18:15-17, 25), and how the Jews too reneged on following Jesus: "And yet there were many who did believe in him, even among the leading men, but they did not admit it, *through fear of the Pharisees and fear of being expelled from the synagogue*: they put honour from men before the honour that comes from God" (John 12:37-43).

Fear makes us look inwards, and in truth we do not like what we see, but it seems better to remain there than to venture outside ourselves to meet the unknown challenge. *Fortitude is a gift of the Spirit of which the fearful stand desperately in need.* Fear makes us afraid to reach out to others, and to be brave enough to be ourselves. We are afraid to stand up and be counted for those things that are dear to us, and conscience dies the slow death of suffocation buried beneath the missed opportunities for personal growth in our lives. Mary became so fearful of being known as a Northern Ireland Catholic that when she came to England she changed her accent, never told anyone where she was from, or what her religion was, and stopped coming to Mass.

I acted like an escaped convict, fearful that someone would discover who I was, and then would follow the most terrible consequences. I was ashamed not so much of my past but of my present lack of courage to be myself. After twice going to your healing Masses I realized that I was letting everyone down, and that fear was crippling my life. When I was released from it the effect was like coming out into the noonday sun.

Mary had very serious emotional problems including acute fits of depression. She also had severe pains in her head and abdomen, all of which disappeared completely once we prayed over her for healing. Since fear affects the whole person then its physical and emotional side-effects are considerable.

Fear of talking about our upbringing because our parents were poor, of the things that really hurt us such as mourning pangs that remain long after the death of a loved one, or the sense of betrayal by people whom we thought were very much part of our lives, do considerable, and sometimes permanent, damage to people. These and other fears have to be brought to light in healing sessions, and the person has to admit to them honestly and bravely. The frightened mind conjures up in the imagination all sorts of calamitous happenings which blind our self-perception. *Fear is a form of psychological blindness.* Its territory is the night, but it soon spills over into the waking hours so that the fearful person walks like someone blindfolded. The bandages have to be taken off *gently*. The fearful person has to believe that God loves him "and has called him out of the darkness into his wonderful light" (1 Peter 2:9). The symptoms of fear have to be described by the person to be healed, as accurately as possible, much as physical pains or disturbances would be to a doctor, or emotional symptoms to a psychiatrist. Gradually, as the hidden fears are brought to light, they lose their power over the person.

The greatest fear is to recognize oneself and to reject what you see. The chapter on "Learning to Love Yourself and Be Healed" says much which is relevant here. Fear hates to be confronted by faith and reality. Like a vampire it sucks our life blood so that we have to unearth the coffin in which it is buried, and drive a stake through the heart of the demon fear. It is only when we recognize fear for what it is that we can begin to be healed of all those other illnesses which up to now were covered over by fear. I have ministered to hundreds, even thousands, of people crippled by fear. Their new lives are a testimony to God's healing power, so that in this life too we might live fully authentic human lives.

Fear, as I said, is basically a lack of faith and hope: we do not believe that God has the power to help us, and even if he did we think that he doesn't really care anyway. We have to get ourselves out of the mess we are in, and we know deep down within ourselves that we just cannot do it. Fear of failure soon gives rise to depression and anxiety. Faith and hope, on the other hand, give us courage to face up to ourselves and to life. Courage is the power of life and its resources within us to assert itself against all the odds. "Though I pass through a gloomy valley, I fear no harm: beside me your rod and your staff are there to hearten me" (Psalm 23:4). In ministering healing to those crippled by fear I assure them always that whatever they find inside themselves, however repulsive it may seem to them, is *already redeemed* by Christ.

The fearful person remains a spiritual infant afraid to face the future with all its bogeys. He can never say "yes" to life because he has not the courage to underwrite himself against what that might entail. Isolated from the world and God, he feels that he must fight his battles alone and unaided. He does not enjoy any sort of freedom, even within himself, where he is at once both prisoner and gaoler. The only way to heal him is to help him break open the rusty, creaking bars of his cell by repeatedly assuring him that God loves him and wants to heal him. There is so much to be written on fear, and of the terrible havoc it has wreaked on people's lives, that it would take volumes to describe it. The minister of healing, when confronted by a fearful person, feels very close to Christ that day in Nazareth when he unrolled the scroll and read "The spirit of the Lord has been given to me to proclaim liberty to captives" (Luke 4:18).

14.

Physical Healing

Jesus in his lifetime on earth was a healer as well as a reconciler. Every time someone who was ill came, or was brought to him, in faith he healed that person of his sickness, whether it was spiritual, emotional or physical. He healed the person and made him whole. This was the object of all healings, whatever their nature. It is a point of fact, and therefore of special significance to his life and mission, that the gospels record him as performing more physical healings than of any other kind. Sickness of the body, which prevented people from living the full human life intended by his Father, was seen by him as part of the kingdom of Satan, which he came to destroy. In order to understand his healing ministry and mission, it would be helpful to read the chapter "Jesus the Wounded Healer", where it sets out that there was no priority in his scale of healing. Healing was very much an essential part of his mission, and therefore *ordinary* to his life. He healed people because he loved them, and knew that this was what his Father wanted him to do.

The Early Church, too, in obedience to its founder, physically healed people, even to the point of raising them from the dead. There is the famous story of Peter raising Tabitha to life when he visited Jaffa. "Peter knelt down and prayed. Then he turned to the dead woman and said, 'Tabitha, stand up'. She opened her eyes, looked at Peter and sat up. Peter helped her to her feet then he called in all the believers and the widows and showed them she was alive. The whole of Jaffa heard about it and many believed in the Lord" (Acts 9:40-42). At Troas, in his travels, Paul restored Eutychus to life after he had fallen from an upstairs window (Acts 10:7-12). Physical healing is so much an essential part of the Gospel of Jesus Christ that to deny it in the Christian Church would be a betrayal of our Christian mission, responsibility and heritage.

Many traditional churches are extremely suspicious of most forms of physical healing and restrict them to special places of pilgrimage, or as evidence of unique holiness in extraordinary people. Physical healing for them is often a challenge to their accepted norms of how God behaves with his Church and people. Spiritual and emotional healing is not only accepted by them, but is so highlighted that any other form of healing is regarded with suspicion and even cynicism. Other churches, especially those most recently established, emphasize physical healing to such an extent that it becomes the criterion of their authenticity as the true Church of Jesus Christ. It claims that those who are not physically healed at their services are lacking in personal faith. These latter churches have witnessed an amazing upsurge in membership, not only in Africa, Asia and South America, but also in these islands and the United States. Physical healing undertaken in the name of the Lordship of Jesus Christ, which should be the source of unity, has become an area of contention and division. This division among the churches is due to a false division and compartmentalalizing of man into soul, emotions and body.

All healing of whatever kind is of the whole person. There is no healing, however physical it may be, which does not affect the emotions and the soul. The example of Joe, whose healing as a person I recalled in the chapter "What is Healing?", is typical of every case of healing in which, together with our team, I have shared. We may be asked to pray for someone with severe pains in the head and discern that we should do so. When that person is healed, even though this may not be immediate, invariably there should be a strengthening of faith and thanksgiving to God, as well as an emotional uplifting of the person's spirit. *No one is ever physically healed just for the sake of physical healing alone. His healing, of whatever kind, is to make him more whole as a person.*

The story of the healing of the Ten Lepers takes into account the spiritual and emotional healing as well as the physical cleansing that took place on the road to Jerusalem. "As Jesus made his way to Jerusalem, he went along the border between Samaria and Galilee. He was going into the village when he was met by ten men suffering from a dreaded skin disease. They stood at a distance and shouted, 'Jesus! Master! take pity on us!' Jesus saw them and said to them 'Go and let the priests examine you'. On the way they were made clean. When one of them saw that he was healed, he came back, praising God in a loud voice. He threw himself to the ground at Jesus' feet and thanked him. The man was a Samaritan. Jesus said, 'There were ten men who were healed; where are the other nine? Why is this foreigner the only one who came back to give thanks to God?' And Jesus said to him, 'Get up and go; your faith has made you well'" (Luke 17:11-19). If we were to concentrate exclusively on the physical healing of the lepers, we should miss many other equally, if not more, vital aspects of the healing narrative. The lepers believed *before* they were physically healed, "On the way they were made clean". One of them, finding himself cured came back "*praising God loudly*". Jesus commended him: "Your *faith* has made you well". All these healings were of the lepers' relationship with God, and were therefore healings of the soul. It was not by chance that the man who returned in gratitude was a Samaritan, and so one can safely presume that among those bystanders to whom Jesus spoke, holding up "this foreigner" as an example, there was a healing of their bigotry and distrust of the Samaritan tribe. The Samaritan "threw himself to the ground at Jesus' feet and thanked him", thereby expressing an emotional healing of one man to another. The nine other lepers who were physically healed were still lacking in their praise to God (soul) and their gratitude to Jesus (emotions). They needed further healing as persons at different levels so that even though they were all physically healed of their leprosy the healing did not have the same effect on them all. *Healing, like persons, is individual.*

What was true on the way to Jerusalem is true of every form of healing which I have been a minister of, or have witnessed. No two healings are alike because no two people are identical. Every form of healing is subordinate and related to the person who is healed. The greatest physical healing may sometimes, as I know only too sadly, produce a seemingly minimal response spiritually in one person, while the smallest physical relief produces outstanding spiritual and emotional reactions in another. In other words, all healing, of whatever nature or dimension, affects the person as a unit. *They are all interactive.* It is always in this sense that I fully accept and engage in the ministry of Christian healing. There is no physical healing for its own sake alone, and this is why I always encourage acts of faith, trust and love of God, and forgiveness of neighbour, *before I begin any ministry of physical healing.* Whenever and wherever I stand before anyone for healing I always pray for the whole person and pray for God to guide our thoughts and prayers. Where there is an over-emphasis on physical healing alone, I am not happy if the dimensions of faith in God and forgiveness of others are omitted. In such cases, I do not pray for physical healing, but for a general healing so that the person's relationships with God, his neighbour and within himself will be healed.

There are physically and emotionally sick people surrounding us on every side, and it is impossible to pray personally and individually for healing for everyone. Many of those who come to me asking just for physical healing alone, and for whom I have no discernment in faith as to the root cause of their sickness, are simply not ready for my ministry. It would be wrong to pretend otherwise, however hurtful this may be to the person concerned. I pray with them for a release of the blockage, but make it clear to them what I am doing. There are others for whom my form of ministry in healing is not suited, either for them as persons, or for their particular illnesses. Doctors and psychiatrists specialize so why shouldn't the Holy Spirit give special aspects of the healing ministry to some and different aspects to others? We are all ministers of his healing power. For me *inner healing* has always been the way the Holy Spirit especially uses my ministry.

Examples help to clarify what I am trying to say. Rebecca came to me for a physical healing of migraine. Her approach was totally selfish: she wanted to be healed because the pain was annoying her. It did not in any way affect her life as a whole person, and I refused to give her anything more than a general blessing. Furious, she went elsewhere for a physical healing, which she claims she received on three occasions, but the migraine returned each time. Eventually she came back to one of our healing sessions, but this time she was prepared to lay her whole life open to the Lord. She had a very strict Catholic upbringing which she resented, and because of his attitude her relationship with her father was bitter, bordering on the hateful. She felt she should come to Mass, but when she left home she stayed away from the church in order to spite her parents. Deep within her she wanted to come, but something inside held her back. She also had two very unhappy love affairs from which she had never fully recovered, and she had lost her self-assurance and respect for herself as a person.

I disliked you intensely (she wrote to me) when you refused to heal me. What right had you to refuse? Were you setting yourself up as a God to decide whom you would heal? I went elsewhere, but I knew the healing was not genuine. It cost me little, and so the nagging doubt remained: Did I want healing and from what? You were right in your discernment that I needed inner peace and healing of memories. It was a painful process looking at my life through the eyes of Christ. But I'm overjoyed I did it. I have made it up with my family, especially with my father, who knew all along apparently that he was too strict. My memory of my misspent youth has been healed and, wonder of wonders, my migraine is gone. My life is fitting together like a pattern, and I think I know what you mean when you talk of the whole person being healed.

The migraine was only a very minor part of Rebecca's healing. She needed to become a whole person.

If physical suffering prevents someone from living a fully human Christian life then such a person should be prayed over for healing. I have written on this in more detail in the chapter "Suffering as a Form of Healing". Physical suffering which is destructive of the person is as great a blockage as personal sin, and should be removed with as much conviction and compassion. Many physical diseases so affect people that they fit into this category. Arthur was such a person and he tells his own story.

Four weeks before attending your service in Preston I was diagnosed as having a chronic leukaemia, and was advised that my best course of action would be to have my spleen removed. If that failed to halt the disease, I would have to undergo chemotherapy. The operation was very, very risky because my spleen had swollen to twelve times its normal size. In between the diagnosis and operation I attended the service for healing, and what made an everlasting impression on me was the complete sense of faith and love of everyone present. To be honest, at first I was embarrassed by this show of complete openness, but gradually it took me over and left me deeply moved. Your words gave me a source of inner strength and a renewed faith in myself, in humanity as a whole and most of all in our Lord Jesus Christ. You laid your hands on me, and I left the church feeling that I could cope with anything that came my way. As for the operation, in the surgeon's own words, he said, "Your spleen fairly jumped out at me. It is an unqualified success." I never suffered any pain, and I was up and walking the same day as I had been operated on. I was released from hospital eight days later, and have been in tremendous health ever since. At the moment there are no traces of bad cells in my blood. The doctors expect me to have a normal life expectancy and I may not even need any further medical treatment. I do not want to minimize the wonderful treatment I received in hospital but I can't stress enough that it was the inner strength I received from your hands which got me through.

Some weeks after receiving his letter I had hoped that Arthur would give his testimony, but he was unable to attend our healing session because he was back at work that day! Leukaemia had virtually destroyed his life at every level. He was a lapsed Catholic, but now his whole life and attitude has changed, to God, to others and to himself, through the physical healing. In his case surgery was used, and I see this as complementary to the Christian healing Arthur received in his whole being through the laying-on of hands. The discernment in faith that we received when praying over Arthur was that he would be converted to the kind of person God the Father wanted him to be. This is the objective of all forms of healing. I am not saying that Arthur's healing was mainly through extraordinary divine intervention, but I am claiming that the laying-on of hands at least triggered off his spiritual and psychological approach to himself and his physical illness. Without this Christian healing aspect it is more than likely that his operation would not have been the unqualified success that it was. All this bears out the theme running through this book, that it is the *person* who is healed.

But there are often more dramatic forms of physical healing which not only dispense with medical science but actually contradict it. Such a case is Joyce who, with her husband Tom, were friends of mine for over a decade. She had suffered grievously with heart complaints and underwent several operations with long periods of convalescence. At least three times her heart had stopped, and those in hospital thought she had died. During these harrowing years she was very much part of my prayer and healing ministry, and was prayed over several times. On these occasions I always advised her to continue with her medical care, until one day when praying over her I was convinced in faith that the Lord would now intervene directly on her behalf, and that there would be no need for further heart surgery. I rarely give this type of advice, in fact, I have done so only four other times, but I was convinced that Joyce was now, after years of pain and surgery, free from her complaint. Let me quote you her letter to me in full.

When you told me a couple of months ago that you would pray that there would be no further heart surgery for me, and that you did not accept the cardiologist's opinion that it was likely, I didn't honestly believe you could be right. I felt so poorly and, to be honest, I didn't really care either. I couldn't see why our Father God had kept me alive and I felt so wretched, I almost wished that He hadn't. It was so selfish of me, of course I realize that Tom was suffering and

I know that you had said that the Lord had a purpose for me, but I didn't recognize it, and anyway I was tired.

During the cardiac catheter investigation, done by local anaesthetic, I was first told that the aortic valve was narrowed and would need major surgery, and then that the right main artery was narrowed also and would need a by-pass operation. My first reaction was, strangely, one of satisfaction. I knew there was something seriously wrong, in spite of your hopeful words to me. The cardiac catheter investigation should have taken about forty-five minutes. In fact I was in theatre a little over two hours. There was plenty of time for my first reaction of satisfaction to fade and something like fear to replace it. I did not relish further surgery. I feared that I would not recover from it this time and I wasn't sure that I wanted to anyway, and I wished that God would arrange to take me "Home" less traumatically.

In consultation with the surgeon, the radiologist found that their first diagnosis was wrong. I wouldn't need any surgery after all. It was decided that the heart pain came from blood clots caused by the artificial mitral valve which my body tried to reject and they would try to control the condition by a variation in the cocktail of heart-drugs that I have to take daily. The pace-maker was working well. So, after four months of hospitalization, investigation and confinement to bed at home, the Almighty Healer had acceded to your prayers on my behalf. Why, I wonder? And what is he wanting to teach me? And how does he want me to live? Tom and I want to live our lives only in accordance with our God's will. That is our joy: but interpreting the Almighty's intention, wishes and direction is not always easy.

Joyce was healed as a person so that she should seek the Lord's will more fully, and accomplish it. Her heart complaint was oppressive and prevented her from helping us as she believed God wanted her to in the ministry of healing. There were times when she came to our meetings in a wheel-chair, a pathetic, pale little figure. Now that she is released from her physical disability she and Tom are able to give us full spiritual, moral and physical support in our healing work. *They have given their lives to the Lord*, and in order to do this more effectively they are completely spiritually in tune with our work for inner healing.

I could write about many more experiences of direct divine intervention in our healing ministry just as compelling as Joyce's healing, but since this book deals essentially with the healing of relationships and the whole person, it is not necessary to devote more space to either physical healing or the healing of memories, false guilt and irrational fear. I have no hesitation in claiming that in our healing sessions there were physical healings of which I have no explanation, other than that they were due to the love of God the Father for his children, whom he made whole so that their lives would be more fully human, fully Christian. I would welcome a medical and psychological examination of any of these people for whom healing is claimed. That which will never show up on an X-ray or scan is the transformation of the person within his whole being. Many doctors and psychiatrists have told me that there is an explanation for every healing that has happened in our sessions, and yet they themselves are unable to effect what we see happen before our eyes when we call on the Lord's name. "If I am not doing my Father's work", said Jesus, "there is no need to believe me; but if I am doing it, then even if you refuse to believe in me, at least believe in the work I do; then you will know for sure that the Father is in me and I am in the Father" (John 10:37-38). No spiritual, emotional or physical disease is outside the scope of Jesus' healing power. He has conquered them all, and in his name lie the victory and the healing.

15.

The Community and Healing

Every Christian community is a healing community for itself, for the Church and for the world. In this very short chapter I want to deal specifically with *a Christian community which comes together in a healing session*. From my own observation and participation in these healing sessions I have found that healing takes place most effectively in a *prayerful, loving community*. The community may be only two or three, but the centre of their consciousness and prayer is the person of Jesus Christ who, in love for us and his Father, reconciles and heals us in whatever way will make us whole. Where the community is small then the immediate family should always, or as far as possible, be involved.

Janine came to us on Good Friday morning, with her mother and father. She was suffering from a disease which doctors and psychiatrists had been unable to identify and treat. She was grossly underweight, and would probably have died but for the physical healing she received that morning. The first part of the session was devoted to encouraging the parents to pray in hope and confidence, and for the mother especially to lose her fear. When the right attitude for healing was reached, I prayed over Janine, whose illness was oppressing her severely, and soon I was convinced that she was completely healed. Six weeks later the mother wrote to me thanking God for what happened to her daughter. Janine is released from the unknown physical disease, and today lives a perfectly normal, healthy life. Her healing has changed the whole family, who gladly acknowledge the power of God's loving intervention.

The healing power of love in a community is typified for me in the healing of a three-year-old girl dying of leukaemia, who was prayed for by the large congregation at one of our healing Masses in Ireland. Her mother brought this frail little girl up to the altar. She looked like a doll with no hair on her head. I encouraged the whole congregation to pray for her and her grieving mother. The atmosphere of love in the church was tangible. Months later the mother brought her daughter, who was completely healed, back to the same church to thank God and the people for their love. "It was your love", she said, "which healed my daughter, and we should all pray in love for each other." Another case in which the power of love in a community was a force for healing, is that of Brian, an eighteen-year-old university student who was suffering from terminal cancer, and for whom his school prayed at Mass, when his whole family was present. The same tangible atmosphere of healing love was present. This year Brian took his finals at university, his cancer totally healed. I have found that where there is no prayer in the community, or too many distractions, then the ministry of healing diminishes in power. We have not yet even begun to understand the spiritual power of a loving, praying, healing, Christian community.

At every healing session, no matter what specific healing is being prayed for, *the community must be expectant* that God the Father will answer our prayers. The words of Jesus on effective prayer (Matthew 6:7-11) are our assurance that every Spirit-filled prayer will be answered by the Father. This expectancy is as natural and right for us today as it was when Jesus walked the roads and streets of Israel, an expectancy that is all too lacking in normal services, and perhaps one of the reasons why so much public prayer seems to go unanswered. On the other hand it is quite wrong, and does untold damage to the individual concerned, and to Christian healing in general, if without true discernment someone is told that he is healed, especially of a physical complaint. Such false hopes are soon replaced by despair, depression and loss of faith when the physical healing does not occur. One thing is certain, namely that some healing, of whatever kind, always takes place where there is loving prayer in an expectant community. *Love always heals*.

Most healings at which our team minister *take place in silence or with a minimum of words*. What God says to us is much more important than what we say to him. Where there is a silence of words, and hearts raised in prayer, it is more likely that we will hear in discerning faith what God is saying to us about the person immediately before us who needs healing. The spirit and atmosphere of prayer in which *everyone* is praising God, and petitioning for healing for someone else, is the ideal setting for the Spirit to work among the Father's people. Obviously, healing sessions attract some people who are too emotional, and so as gently but as firmly as possible we try to prevent any unnecessary noise intruding on the quiet waiting on the Lord which is part of all our healing services. I have been to sessions conducted by other ministers in which there was a lot of shouting and near hysteria, and however well-intentioned it may be, I find that I cannot relate to it in my spirit. Where someone needs healing in which it is foreseen that a high level of noise and emotion will be involved, then it would seem better to deal with such cases privately, and in *very small experienced groups*. The shouting can cause distress to people in the congregation as well as being a distraction from deep prayer.

In order to preserve the prayerful atmosphere, it is usual for us to have someone lead a meditation with periodic, gentle singing of hymns with appropriate healing words. The essential thing to remember is that these prayers should be short, truly inspired by the Spirit, and with long periods of silence. On a few occasions the healing was not helped by someone praying for Northern Ireland, the Third World and every conceivable social problem under the sun! The presence of God as a gentle, healing, loving Father is often buried beneath purely human sound and unbridled emotion. *Listen to the Spirit and he will never fail to speak the Father's loving word to us*. The motto for all healers is "Whenever possible don't say it, pray it". The words of the Spirit are always few, powerful and healing.

The healing community must be, above all, *thankful*. Thankfulness is the keynote of Jesus' prayers of healing even before the healing takes place, such as in the raising of Lazarus from the dead. "Father, I thank you for hearing my prayer" (John 11:41). His farewell discourses recorded in John 14-17 are redolent with praise and glory to God his Father. Whether or not we are aware of it, *in every healing session healing takes place*, and we should thank and praise our loving Father for it. In the praising itself there is contained the source of even more healing. Far too often, people come selfishly for healing for themselves, and their minds are so preoccupied with their own complaints that they pull the spiritual tone of the service down to one of selfish petition, or a kind of spiritual greed. They are like the nine lepers who forgot to return and give thanks to Jesus for their healing.

There is little point in services beginning with people saying repeatedly, and rather mindlessly, "We praise you, Lord, we thank you Lord", if their minds and hearts are elsewhere, especially if they are centred on themselves. Thanksgiving should follow some sort of loose pattern such as praising God as our Father, Jesus for being one of us, the Spirit for enriching us, and finally for all the gifts we have in our lives. When we remember how much we have been given then we will be more ready to pray for others. Martin, who is blind, is always full of praise for the good things in his life, and is a source of healing for those around him. Just as there is a power failure when the electrical system is over-loaded, so also healing diminishes to the point of near extinction where prayers are overloaded with petition rather than praise and thanksgiving. In ministering to people, especially where I discover strong overtones of selfishness or self-pity, I always ask them to pray in thanksgiving for what they have received. Where there is no spirit of thanksgiving, I find it impossible to proceed with any healing other than encouraging them to look at their lives, and appreciate all that is positive in it.

The healing community is *patient*. Instant healing is not always the pattern of our services. Often the healing is gradual and not always of the type that was prayed for. The Spirit moves us to pray in a certain way but the Father, understanding the "words" of the Spirit, will heal those areas which are most seriously affecting the wholeness of the person. Time and again people have come for physical healing, and received inner healing instead. On reflection, perhaps days later, they will come to appreciate that this was really the type of healing they needed. Too often, people claim a physical healing whereas something much more beautiful happened inside them, which is a source of strength for the rest of their lives.

Brian, for example, claimed a physical healing from cancer which had riddled his body, and for a time was convinced of this healing. What he was really healed of was his obsessive fear of cancer and dying, and his guilt over his past life. Months later he died serenely in his sleep, at peace with God, his family and within himself. I did not for a moment consider his healing to be a failure, nor did it prevent him from doing the things he wanted to do. He lived life to the full, in the best sense of the word, up to the day he died. Our obsession with physical healing has done much to limit the whole area of healing to the body, forgetting that it is the whole person who needs healing.

Finally, the community must be *open* to the Lord. There is little point in having a healing service in which we have already come with our "package of requests". The prayer which opens us to God always heals. Recently I went to a healing service in which a very high proportion of people present were physically and mentally handicapped. The mood at the beginning was for the physical healing, mainly arising from relations and friends of those who had brought their sick to the service. It soon changed to thanksgiving and praise of such a deep spiritual quality as I have rarely experienced elsewhere. I am saddened by many people who, for themselves or for others, are so seemingly irreversibly obsessed with physical healing that they miss out on developing the inner qualities of soul and emotions of the whole person. I know of one lady who travelled incessantly to "all the shrines and healers of Europe" for the relief of her complaint, but who finally received the inner healing of peace at a healing Mass in Tadcaster, a mere ten miles from her own home. The community that remains open to the Father will be flooded with his healing love. We could ask for, or receive, nothing better.

16.

The Church and Healing

The Church is the body of Christ. Its life and teaching is his. We will recognize and identify the True Church because in word and deed it enshrines the teaching and actions of its founder. Who and what is the Church? The Church is the sharing of the faithful in the life of its risen Lord, with all the various gifts of the Spirit, so that Christ's life may be seen to be active in his Church. "Now you together are Christ's body; but each of you is a different part of it. In the Church, God has given the first place to apostles, the second to prophets, the third to teachers; after them, miracles, and after them the gift of healing, helpers, good leaders, those with many languages" (1 Corinthians 12:27-28).

Every facet of Jesus' life is to be found in the Church. The Gospel comes alive in Christian believers as individuals and as a community. Jesus gave generously to his followers so that whatever he did, so could they. In fact, he promised that "we would do greater things" so that the world might learn to believe. As Jesus laid his hands on the sick to heal them, so does the Church. As he reconciled sinners to the Father and to the community, so do Christian believers. As he gave thanks to his Father and shared with others the bread and wine which were his body and blood, so do we. We see marriage as the sacred union of husband and wife which the Church blesses in a unique way because of Jesus' teaching on marriage, and because he worked his first miracle at the wedding feast of Cana. We, in the Church's Sacraments, do these and other wonderful healing actions in memory of Christ in order to make his presence effective, and life-saving among his people. Such is the general Catholic approach to healing.

This book concentrates on healing alone. The healings of Jesus formed *the major part* of his public life. His essential teaching was enshrined in his healing. He loved people because he was the incarnate, human, Son of God, and he healed them because he loved them. His healing contained the evidence and message that God the Father loved us, and wanted everyone to be reconciled and healed. The reason for the healing mission of Jesus was twofold; his own compassion for others, and his obedience to the will of his Father who loved and cared about his people, diseased and weakened by sin. The Church today has the same message of love and obedience to the loving Father's healing, saving will, *and so the Church is a healing community*. It is in how the various churches interpret the meaning of "healing" that grave misunderstandings occur.

The healings of Jesus were not a temporary phase in salvation history which are now nothing more than an historical fact. Nor are the gospels a chronicle of past events in the "golden age" of its founder. Healing is as essential to the message of the Church today as it was to that of Jesus, so that the Good News of liberation, reconciliation, and the making whole of every human person, may help people to believe that Jesus is the Lord sent to us by our loving Father. In his world Jesus encountered cynicism, disbelief, jealousy, fatalism, apathy and all those destructive human elements to which our fallen human nature is prone. Our world today is arguably more secular and pagan than in Jesus' own lifetime, and consequently the Church needs to exercise the gifts of the Spirit given to it as vigorously and fully as it can. My own personal faith in the divine power enshrined in the person of Jesus Christ is not solely based on the healings which took place two thousand years ago. Rather it is enlivened and enriched by the great things which are happening today in the Church, as it performs healings so special that those who witness and experience them see the person of Christ, and the power of his Gospel, come alive as dramatically as at any time during Jesus' own short lifetime on earth.

That the Early Church was a healing Church does not require any confirmation from me. Jesus knew that healing was an essential part of the message of salvation, just as essential as reconciliation, and that is why he gave his disciples power to heal when he sent them out to preach the Gospel. "He called the twelve together and gave them power and authority over all devils and to cure diseases, and he sent them out to proclaim the Kingdom and to heal" (Luke 9:1-2). The proclamation of the Kingdom and the power to heal were concomitant: one was the trumpet of the other's message. The power to heal was equally given to the seventy-two disciples and for the same purpose: "Cure those who are sick and say 'The Kingdom of God is very near to you'" (Luke 10:9-10). Jesus linked the preaching of his doctrine with the power to heal so that people believed in his message because of the healing power which accompanied it. The healing enshrined the message of love. Jesus promised to everyone who believed in him that "he will perform the same works as I do myself; he will perform even greater works because I am going to the Father" (John 14:12). This power was exercised most frequently and effectively in the Early Church. Their preaching of Christ's rising from the dead, and the sending of his Holy Spirit, was accompanied by healing of such power that it was obvious that God the Father's love and presence was with them.

There is no indication in the gospels that this healing ministry of Jesus would shrink, or even end after his physical life on earth. On the contrary it was expected, as in the Early Church, that it would increase and intensify as those who believed in future ages would obey Christ's command "Go out to the whole world; proclaim the Good News to all creation. And these will be the signs that will be associated with believers; they will lay their hands on the sick who will recover" (Mark 16:16-18). One of the main reasons, perhaps, why some churches have not grown spiritually and numerically as they should in recent times, or been demonstrably filled with the power of the Holy Spirit, is that there has been a shrinking in faith of their followers. They have set aside, to a large extent, the ministry and apostolate of healing. People outside the Church will not believe in doctrine alone which is not saturated with the healing power of Jesus Christ. If we had the faith necessary for the ministry of Christian healing, then the healings would follow as surely as they did when St Peter met the man who was a cripple from birth and said, "I have neither silver nor gold, but I will give you what I have: in the name of Jesus Christ the Nazarene, walk!" (Acts 3:6).

The healings of Jesus and the Early Church were not designed to build up an institutional church of such proportions that there would come a time when healings were no longer necessary to proclaim the Gospel, or to further the mission of the Church. We have only to look around us at our Sunday congregations to appreciate how much need there is today for Christian healing. People come to church hungry for a God living among them. They seek healing, and if the local church fails them many will travel hundreds, even thousands, of miles to some shrine or sacred place dedicated to healing, not so much for physical healing but to strengthen their belief in a God who cares. If we preached more often, and with the conviction which comes from a living faith, on healing in its fullest sense of making a person whole in soul, emotions and body, then those troubled in faith, tormented by memories or crippled in body would fill to over-flowing the greatest and smallest church buildings. There would be "no more room left even in front of the door" (Mark 2:2). Our small church in Tadcaster holds three hundred people when extra chairs are brought in for special occasions. At our last healing Mass, which was only the eighth since we started, over five hundred people spilled over on to the lawn and street outside. Even though we had no loud-speaker system, those outside refused to go away and remained praying because they knew, sensed, that God was healing his people and they wanted to be near.

There is a great deal of talk of renewal in the Church today, and I believe that it will come about, not through an intellectual grasp of doctrine, but through a spiritual power of healing which makes that doctrine come alive in people's personal lives. People sigh in longing for this great healing power to be unleashed again today in our church and world. Let me quote from a letter. Shirley, of Middlesex, is one of our group who helps in the ministry of healing, and she wrote:

So many times I decide not to come again to the healing meetings but I always end up there. I had decided this time to spend the day in a *Poustinia* fasting and praying for you and the meeting, but because the weather has been so cold they are not opening the *Poustinia* until April. I knew I would find the meeting painful. I feel so helpless and there are so many: blind Martin, autistic Gerard, Shaun crippled with arthritis, Katrina paranoid, John, Paul – I could go on and on and we have prayed for years for so many of them. I look around me at the meetings and see the unspoken pleading in everyone's eyes. Most don't even know how to express what they need, but the silent cry is there – "Notice me, help me. I'm not crippled or blind but I am still in pain". How do you cope with all that? I don't think I can. I can't think why the Lord wants me there. This is the trouble with growing in the spiritual life. God is so beautiful, but you have to see too what is not Him; you have to face the emptiness of where he is not. It makes me afraid to go on, and yet you can't turn back, and you can't stand still either. I believe God is calling me closer to him but I find myself drawing back, partly because I dare not approach the beauty of him, and partly because I don't think I can handle it when you have to look away. Let no one believe that to grow in the Lord is to float on a rosy cloud.

Shirley, like all Christian healers, is wounded and the secret of her healing ministry is her compassion. As a Christian she is aware that many people are so crippled in soul, mind and body that they are unable to live the full Christian life as God our Father intended they should. Shirley, therefore, believes in healing of every kind which will set people free to live the new life of the Holy Spirit. Renewal in the Church and world will come about when we all, of whatever Christian denomination, turn back to God our loving Father and ask for healing.

For over ten years I organized many high-powered, theological, scriptural, liturgical, social and moral conferences as Director of Wood Hall Centre in Yorkshire, but I now see such conferences alone, without healing, as dressing up a wounded body in fine clothes without ever getting down to the nature of the disease. In a world so flagrantly violent, divided and sick, it is only right that various Christian churches should at last begin to encourage a more open and understanding attitude to the whole question of healing. No church has a monopoly of Christian healing and I, like many thousands of others, have experienced healing at the hands of Christians who did not belong to my church. "John said to Jesus, 'Master, we saw a man who is not one of us casting out devils in your name; and because he was not one of us we tried to stop him'. But Jesus said, 'You must not stop him: no one who works a miracle in my name is likely to speak evil of me. Anyone who is not against us is for us'" (Mark 9:38-40). The Holy Spirit is not the exclusive possession of any one group of Christians at the expense of others in the distribution of his gifts. The Spirit, the great source of unity and power in the Church, uses people of all shades of Christian affiliation to make the Kingdom of God come on earth. Christian healing is at once a great source of evangelization and of unity. When the various churches and their members will be healed of their divisions and distrust, then, after centuries of waiting, the world will witness again a healing power at work as never before since the glorious days of the Early Church. I believe that Christian healing, far from being a source of division between Christians, will become the power-base of Christian unity and mission.

Every healing session at which our group ministers is ecumenical, in what I hope is the best sense of the word. God is our Father who has no favourites. We all remain open to the Spirit, and after years of working for Christian unity at so many other levels, I am amazed at the barriers broken down, the bridges built, through our common healing. It is truly wonderful how the Lord literally becomes the peace between us as the institutional tunnel-vision of so many good people is widened to horizons of the Kingdom. Our healing sessions do not have to contrive an ecumenical flavour because we believe from experience that it is the Spirit who is speaking and active through each one of us, regardless of our ecclesiastical "colouring". John, a leader in his Protestant Evangelical community, and a sharer with us in our healing sessions, wrote to me saying, "I come to a healing service because I know Christ is there working among us, not so much bringing us together but bringing us to the Father. I have come to know the Spirit better through Catholics because I have heard him speak through them. This healing of our divisions is quite unique. How can you possibly be at enmity with someone whom the Father loves and on whom the Spirit has abundantly poured his blessings? Of course, we still disagree on doctrine and a thousand and one other things, but shared healings has changed our attitudes. Surely this is what Christian love is all about and how we were meant to live."

As well as the ecumenical dimension, Christian healing begins in each Christian church and community. There is no Church which is not in constant need of healing. No institution, however inspired its origins may be, is above reproach, and if its leaders think it is perfect, then they themselves need healing of spiritual arrogance and complacency. Maureen, through her healing, became aware of the great truths of the Christian faith enshrined in the Roman Catholic Church of which she has been a loyal and totally dedicated member for many years.

When I went to Sunday Mass after my first healing, I wanted to tell everyone what the Lord had done for me. The sad thing was that no one wanted to listen. I am not a charismatic – just an ordinary Christian! But I now know how beautiful the Mass and the Sacraments of the church are. It is as if each day is my very first as a Catholic and Christian. I loved my church before, now it is a source of joy to me. I pray every day for all my family and my whole parish to be healed of their apathy and complacency.

Maureen's family has been healed and renewed, and it is a triumph of God's grace to see the joy and happiness shining out of their faces. Hundreds of Catholics and Protestants have returned to a *living* practice of their faith after receiving healing from God the Father through his Son. The dull routine of the Sunday services has been lit up by a spiritual understanding of what thanksgiving, praise, adoration and healing are all about. "I felt a stranger among my own family and parish at first", said Maureen, "but I was filled with a patience and inner strength which saw me through. I did not want to be different from them, and yet I was. In a sense the waiting for their healing has been a further source of healing to me."

Today the various Christian churches and ecclesiastical communities are investigating, spiritually and practically, the implications of healing. In my own church there has been a liturgical renewal in healing since the Second Vatican Council which ended two decades ago, but this liturgy has still to find its way into the spiritual bloodstream of Catholics. For Catholics the main sources of healing are the Sacraments, and the seeds of great spiritual healing and renewal have been sown there through the thinking and statements of the Second Vatican Council. The growing emphasis on the central role of the resurrection of Jesus Christ, who is Lord of our Christian lives, has had a profound and renewing effect on our understanding of the nature and function of the Church. As Christians we Catholics are "an Easter people and alleluia is our song". It is in the sense of being "in Christ" which prompted us to a deepening of our perception of the meaning and significance of the Sacraments. We "celebrate" – what a joyful, healing word of freedom – all the Sacraments in the risen Lord because above everything else the ultimate triumph of Christ has pride of place in our lives and religious practices. In Christ there is no spiritual death, only healing, and through him we triumph. Our concern is always and everywhere in the Sacraments to express our living hope through the resurrection. The cross takes its place in our lives, but we are no longer a cross-centred people who see suffering as an end in itself. Those outside the Roman Catholic community would do well to pray about and study the spiritual and theological thinking of Catholics today, so that they may realize how healed and renewed they have become. Here are some of the Catholic attitudes to the Sacraments, based on their Church's statements and practice.

Baptism is not just the negative washing away of sin, but the Sacrament of new life that comes to us through our death in Christ so as to be *born again*. It is a Sacrament of resurrection in so far as it signifies new life from death, and is the promise of our own resurrection in Christ. What we need to encourage in our people is an awareness of all that this means in their lives. Jack and Joan had two children baptized without giving much thought to it. Then they came to a healing service, and the change was remarkable.

As we prepared for Louise's birth, my third and rather "unexpected" baby, there was an atmosphere of joy at the new life coming into our family. When she was born and just before the actual baptismal service, we prayed and fasted as a family. We all took part in the service and what a joy it was for all. Our other two children were baptized in the same church by the same priest using the same words, but this time it was different. I suppose it was because we were healed and knew how close Christ was to us on that day.

What a beautiful letter from Joan! The best form of preparation and instruction for baptism will always remain healing, so that parents' ears and hearts will be open to the healing power of baptism by which we are born again. I am sure that Jack and Joan will take Louise along the Christian path so that when she grows older she will also grow spiritually and remain always a new Christian. *In my language, Christians are born every day and remain as fresh as newly baked bread.* Those who do not share over Catholic faith do not always appreciate that for us Baptism is very much a healing sacrament because it is directed against sin, including original sin, the source of all forms of sickness and death.

The Sacrament of **Confirmation** is another healing, Spirit-filled Sacrament. The risen Lord whose life we share, through baptism sends his Spirit upon us and we are called to be witnesses to the Kingdom of God. In our healing services we always anoint or bless the hands of those who want to pray for the sick, or who wish to be strengthened in their resolve to live out the Gospel in their daily lives. I believe that this healing is very important to remind people of their Christian vocation and commitment in Confirmation. Much more could be made of this Sacrament in a healing context, and I pray that thought and prayerful action will help our people to achieve in practice what the Sacrament signifies.

The **Eucharist**, or the Mass, has always been the centre of my Catholic, liturgical and spiritual life. It is the great healing event in which Christ meets me in the community in a personal encounter and fills me with his life. The healing side of the Sacrament has in the past been largely overlooked. Its whole structure is so arranged as to express what we feel towards God our Father, who sent us his Son as our healer so that our sins might be taken away, and his Spirit to fill us with his gifts and power at every healing session. Wherever possible, I offer Mass as the centre-piece around which all the healing, praise and petition take place.

The healing Mass for me (wrote Brenda) says it all. The confession of our sins, the hearing of God's word, the presence of Christ, the sign of peace, the communion, the sheer happiness of being with other Christians who believe and feel as I do, is in itself, every time, a healing for me. If only all Masses were like that, then our churches would be so packed you would not be able to get into them. It has changed my attitude to Mass and my

Church. I feel as if I have come fully alive for the first time in my life. The full healing power of the Mass has not been released to our people. Why?

We, however spiritual we may feel, are surrounded on all sides by sin. Even though we have been redeemed and reconciled to the Father, we are still conscious that we live in a sin-filled world. We are only too well aware of our own personal weakness. We need the Father's healing love and protection lest we fall, and fall we do, however loudly other Christians insist that "you can't fall if you're saved". When we sin and, like the Prodigal Son, we wish to return to our Father's home, we come before him to ask his mercy. God the Father welcomes the sinner back home, and heals him of his past ingratitudes and selfishness. It is in Christ that we are reconciled to God the Father through his mystical body of the Church. The mercy of the Father, uniquely revealed in the life, death and resurrection of Jesus Christ, remains for ever in his Church. "For those whose sins you forgive, they are forgiven; for those whose sins you retain, they are retained" (John 20:23). Instead of calling it the Sacrament of Penance or Confession, we now call it the Sacrament of **Reconciliation**. Reconciliation is really a "change of heart" or "conversion" for the sinner. The healing that should flow from this Sacrament is often drastically reduced, not only because of the impersonal nature in which the Sacrament is administered, but because it deals mainly with matters of the soul and not with the healing of the whole person. It is the *whole person* who is reconciled and healed through this Sacrament. Whenever, in our healing services we emphasize the healing needed for conversion, it is quite amazing to discover how many people wish to receive the sacrament of reconciliation in order to start a "new life", or have a "fresh beginning".

Healing gives people the will and the power to change

their life-style, and put right our relationship with God, our neighbour and within ourselves. Matthew was an alcoholic and no matter how he tried, he could not break the habit. We were led to pray over him and I discerned that he was healed of his addiction. "I knew that I was healed," he wrote, "but I needed something more. I wanted to be assured that my past sins and the hurts I had done to other people were forgiven. As a Catholic I wanted to make a really good confession and start a new life. The healing released my soul, and I made the best confession in my life." This may sound Catholic talk and therefore meaningless jargon to other Christians, but it certainly meant everything to Matthew. I met him a few weeks ago and he is a completely renewed, healed person.

The sacrament of **Matrimony** is also a great healing source of Christ's love for those who feel called as man and woman to share their lives together. It is the community Sacrament of Christ's Church on earth. "Husbands should love their wives just as Christ loved the Church" (Ephesians 5:25). In our healing sessions we emphasize the need for true sharing and commitment to each other. Such a couple were Jerome and Elizabeth, who in the eyes of their neighbours were a very happily married couple, yet there were deep hurts between and within them which prevented their life together being as full of love as it should be. Elizabeth spoke openly and honestly about their problem.

We got married in our teens and we didn't really understand what marriage was all about. We never talked deeply to each other about our childhood or what we wanted from life. We married, had a family, but we did not grow together as persons. We both felt we needed to really communicate with each other but we didn't know how. We went to Marriage Guidance counsellors and the lot, but they never got through to the real source of our pain. We knew that we needed a higher force or power to crack us open. This happened to us both at one of your healing services. Suddenly we both knew we needed healing. It was, as you know, a long, slow painful process in which both Jerome and I felt the need to change. We were sustained not so much by our children or any advice we received but by the Holy Spirit who entered our lives and changed us. The rest, you know. We came to your last healing session to renew our marriage commitment, and this time it really meant something. I think we both have a clearer understanding now of what marriage is all about, but hasn't it taken a long time and the Holy Spirit to heal us?

There are many like Jerome and Elizabeth who need healing in marriage, but often one or both parties are not prepared to pay the price. The correct time for healing in marriage is *before* not after it. Young couples who are serious in their intentions about Christian marriage would benefit immeasurably from a healing session with other couples. By "healing session" I do not mean guidance, counselling or any thing which is short of being completely spiritual and orientated towards the healing of the whole person of both parties and their future relationship.

The Church in its early days did not confine healing to the priesthood. The commissioning to heal was a special charism. Yet even the most cursory glance at the ordination service of a priest, or the manner in which he is regarded by Catholics in relation to the Sacraments, shows that today *the priest is expected to be a healer*. If he is encouraged to administer the Sacraments in such a way that their healing content is emphasized then truly this sacrament of Holy Orders will come alive again in a healing, charismatic rather than a functionary way. When priests understand the true nature of healing, which in the minds of so many Catholics is linked with their office, then a great spring of healing will flow more easily through the Catholic community. I have always regarded my duties as a priest as involving me in healing, but in recent years the words "priest" and "healing" have taken on a new meaning and dimension.

Of course, the Sacrament to undergo the greatest, most radical change in Catholic thinking and practice, has been the Sacrament of the **anointing of the sick**. Previously it was called "Extreme Unction" or "the Last Rites". For many centuries it brought great inner peace to those who received it and, I am sure, helped them to depart this life in a very tranquil way, which also brought comfort to their nearest and dearest. There were times too when there was a noticeable physical improvement, even to the extent of a complete recovery. However, the emphasis was on the person's final preparation for his journey home to God, and there was a finality about a priest coming with the oils into a sick room. It was a signal that death was not far away, and often it was the priest's task to break the news to the patient, and, if needs be, to his loved ones.

All that has now changed. The new name of the Sacrament, "Anointing of the Sick", means exactly what it says, and it has developed very *strong overtones of healing* in keeping with the practice of the Early Church as interpreted for us by the Epistle of James. "If one of you is ill, he should send for the elders of the church and they must anoint him with oil in the name of the Lord and pray over him. The prayer of faith *will save* the sick man and the Lord *will raise him up again*; and if he has committed any sins they *will be forgiven*" (James 5:14-15). The emphasis is on the healing of the whole person, and while it would be wrong to so over-emphasize physical healing that everything else is neglected and pushed to the periphery, nevertheless it is one of the ends of the Sacrament. Today when I administer the Sacrament I pray for the healing of the whole person, and in the spirit, if I am led to, then I have no hesitation in praying for physical healing. Last Maundy Thursday, when I was present at the Blessing of the Oils by the Bishop of our diocese, I noticed how many times he used the word "healing" over the oils. When he blessed the Oil of the Sick he said, "May your blessing come upon all who are anointed with this oil that they may be freed from pain, illness and disease and made well again in body, mind and soul." Our priests and people have yet to absorb this radical teaching fully into their system, but there is no doubt that, liturgically and sacramentally, healing of the whole person is very much a part of the Catholic Church's attitude to sickness.

Catholics find their main source of healing within the Sacraments, but *it should not be the only one*. We have a lot to learn about the gifts and the ministries of the spirit. When we do, then the words used in all our sacramental rites will take on a new, deeper and more vital meeting. In a truly Gospel sense, as Catholics, we are learning to become better Christians, and in the process we find something new and glorious in our faith every day of our lives. It would be a betrayal of our Christian tradition if we were to underrate the importance and effectiveness of the sacraments as sources of Christian healing, but when we widen our spiritual horizons and become more open to the Holy Spirit, our sacraments will become truly living personal contacts with the healing Christ. They will be his touch and not something which produces its effect *ex opere operato*, independent of our faith, and our uniqueness as persons who want to touch even the "fringe of his cloak".

Those churches or ecclesiastical communities which so over-emphasize physical healing to the neglect of the spiritual dimension of the whole person who needs healing, have also a great deal to learn. Books on healing which are nothing other than a chronicle of physical signs and wonders leave a great deal to be desired, because as they raise expectancy and often times false hopes, they also minimize the totality of the human person. Mass-produced physical healing in large assembly halls finds no echo in the Gospel, where even in crowds the healings were person to person or in small groups. They disturb the spiritual depths of the souls of many Christians who discard healing because of the "show-biz type" of some of the glamorous healers. We are all members of the Church of Christ, and while we must recognize each other's gifts we must also be sensitively aware of the promptings of the Spirit and the presence of his gifts and ministries in other groups. What really offends Catholics is the *exaggerated* emphasis on deliverance and exorcism, and the manner in which it is performed by some healing groups. These remarks are made in charity, because we all have so much to learn from the Spirit and from each other.

We are the Body of Christ on earth. "Just as the human body, though it is made up of many parts, is a single unit because all these parts, though many, make one body, so it is with Christ. . . . Nor is the body to be identified with any one of its many parts. If the foot were to say, 'I am not a hand and so I do not belong to the body', would that mean that it stopped being part of the body? . . . Instead of that, God put all the separate parts into the body on purpose. If all the parts were the same, how could it be a body? As it is, the parts are many but the body is one. The eye cannot say to the hand, 'I do not need you', nor can the head say to the feet, 'I do not need you'" (1 Corinthians 12:12, 14-15,18-21).

We all need each other in the Christian churches so that Christ's healing power may be made manifest in us through the healing within and between our communities, in order that as members of the Church we may fulfil our healing mission to a wounded world. We have a long road to travel, but at least we have started on the way. Every healing within the Church heals us all, because it is our brothers and sisters who are healed.

17.

Prayers for Healing

For Healing Power

God, our Father, you sent your only Son, Jesus, on earth to heal a broken-hearted and wounded world. He had compassion on those who called on him for help and healing. He touched the sick and guilt-laden, and they walked away in health and freedom of Spirit. Visit us now with his saving power so that we too may be released in mind and body to praise your healing grace, through Christ our Lord.*

God, our Father, your Son gave more than he was asked for to those who pleaded with him for healing. People asked for health of body and he released them from their sins as well; he touched their skin and healed the deep wounds of the spirit. May we be touched by the same healing power and thus be released from the hidden forces deep within us, which hold us back from true health of mind and body.*

Jesus, your coming on earth was like a new dawn over a world of darkness: the blind saw, the lame walked again, the sick were healed and even the dead were raised to life. Come again into the lives of everyone and heal the wounds of their broken hearts. Come again to all who are sick or depressed and fill their lives with hope and peace. Come again to us as we call on your holy name, so that we too may receive your help and healing grace.*

God, our Father, I turn to you in my unrest because I cannot see any way out of the present situation which

221

troubles my spirit. In my confusion I turn to you for help and guidance, because you alone can help me and nothing is impossible to you. Light up my life with faith, strengthen me in hope and fill me with love, so that I may rest in your providence, which alone knows what is for my peace.*

Lord Jesus, you are the great friend of the sick
and you healed them while you were on earth.
Grant them once more your healing power and
comfort them in their affliction.
Come Holy Spirit, strengthen them so that they may
find renewed health
both in soul and body.*

For Doctors, Nurses and All those who Care for the Sick*

Lord Jesus, wounded healer of all those who are wounded in our weary world, you who knew the caring love of holy people who helped you in your distress, be with, and bless, all those who care for the sick and disabled. Give patience to their minds, peace to their hearts, so that in tending the sick they will know it is you, our wounded healer, whom they touch and heal with your saving power.

For the Gift of Sleep

Lord Jesus Christ, who slept on a storm-tossed lake, grant me the gift of sleep so that with a mind at peace, a heart at rest, and a body relaxed, I may use my sleeping hours for healing, and waken strengthened to renew my tasks with brighter vision, confidence and hope.

Resignation in Illness

God, you are a loving Father who will not cause us a needless tear; give us then a peaceful heart at rest in the present trouble which afflicts us and which we offer to you in union with the sufferings of Christ, your Son. May we concentrate more on your love and care, rather than on our own selfish preoccupation with physical pain and emotional disturbance. You know the right time to lift the burden that oppresses us and so we place the present moment, as we do our whole lives, in your tender care. Put your rest in our minds and your peace in our hearts.

For the Correct Use of Suffering*

Father, you want to heal us, and make us whole, but we live in a world damaged by sin. We feel within us the pains of alienation from you, from our neighbour and from what we ourselves should be. Be with us now in the present suffering which afflicts us, and send your healing peace into the midst of all our pain. We cannot be, or live, at peace by our own unaided efforts, so send your Spirit upon us that we may know that in all the storms which surround us, you are with us as we offer to you all our sufferings, in union with the loving obedience of Jesus, your only Son, our Lord.

Father, we offer you in union with Jesus in the Garden of Gethsemane, a heart that trusts you in the dark, and a mind at rest in your loving arms, so that when the dawn comes we may know that you have always been there supporting, strengthening and healing us.

A Spirit of Thanksgiving

God, whose mercy is boundless and whose gifts are without end, help us always to thank you for everything that your loving power has bestowed upon us. Make us realize that our desire to thank you is itself your gift, and that our thankfulness is never-ending because your love is never-failing.

All prayers taken from *The Treasury of the Holy Spirit*, except those marked *, which the author composed for this book.